The Horse Show Mom's
Survival
Guide

The Horse Show Mom's
Survival
Guide

BY SUSAN S. DANIELS

Illustrations by Harry Weber

The Lyons Press
Guilford, Connecticut
An imprint of The Globe Pequot Press

The Lyons Press is an imprint of The Globe Pequot Press

10 9 8 7 6 5 4 3 2

Printed in the United States of America

Designed by Maggie Peterson

ISBN 1-59228-394-2

Library of Congress Cataloging-in-Publication data is available on file.

For my husband, Bob,
with love and deep appreciation

Contents

Acknowledgments		ix
Introduction		xi
1	First Things First	1
2	What to Expect	9
3	The Barn Universe	21
4	The Trainer	35
5	Buying and Selling Your Horse or Pony	53
6	Here Comes the Judge	67
7	Horse Show Dads	73
8	Western Breeds	79
9	Hunter/Jumpers and Equitation	111
10	Dressage	147
11	Eventing	167
12	It's Not Soccer	193
Appendix I A: American Quarter Horse Association		197
Appendix I B: American Paint Horse Association		201
Appendix I C: Appaloosa Horse Club		205
Appendix I D: Pony of the Americas		207
Appendix I E: Pinto Horse Association of America		211
Appendix I F: Arabian Horse Association		215
Appendix II A: Hunter/Jumper Organizations		217
Appendix II B: Points		219
Appendix II C: Indoors and Other National Horse Shows		227
Appendix II D: Jumper Tables		235
Appendix II E: The Marshall and Sterling League Finals		237
Appendix III: Eventing Points		239
Glossary		243
Resources		251
Index		253

Acknowledgments

It is with deep gratitude that I would like to thank the following people for all manner of help that was given me during the writing of this book: Harry Weber for his delightful drawings, and more for his willingness to share his talent with me; Ann Weber for her extensive knowledge and thorough editing skills; my editor Steve Price for knowledge, help, and the right amount of prodding; Jessie Shiers, production editor for The Lyons Press, for pulling it all together; Jill Paxton for invaluable support and help with the Western breeds chapter; Jose Moreno of the AQHA; Sharon Gallagher of the USEA, for the many hours of sharing her knowledge of eventing; and the same for Jill Williams and Jenny Burkhardt; Lendon Gray for all things dressage, given with such generosity; Susan Dotson of the USEF for reading, over and over, the Hunter/Jumper chapter and giving me advice; and Carol and Harvey Coleman for support and encouragement.

For the use of their professional photographs, I would like to thank Richard Hildreth and K.C. Montgomery.

For all of the kind people who responded to my cold-calling or impromptu interviews for information: Sandy Arledge, Jenny Forsberg Meyer, Sue Copeland, Beth Miner, Bonnie Watchover, Carrie Zahradnik, Suzie Drish, Ginny Cantwell of the APHA office, Missy Corn at the POAC, Keely Gant of the Appaloosa Horse Club, Holly Davis and Theresa Pruitt of the Pinto Horse Association, Mary Creech of the Marshall and Sterling League, Sarah Ike of USEF's High Performance Division, Caroline Vincent of the National Horse Show, Sheila Forbes of the USDF, and Kelly Blair and Patricia Sutter for sharing their Arabian knowledge, I give my thanks.

A special thank you goes to Mandy Lorraine for appreciating and encouraging my writing.

I would also like to express my deep appreciation to the Bate family—Ken, Johnna, Kendall, and Jordy—who so kindly housed us during the Winter Circuit in Wellington, Florida, giving me a great opportunity for firsthand research, plus a lovely place to write.

In addition, all of the horse show moms, dads, and equestrian kids who read my chapters and offered input and support, have my permanent affection: Bob Daniels, #1 horse show dad; Chetana Daniels, this family's horse show kid; Ben Daniels; and Genevra Williams, astute readers and critics all. I also thank Claudia Turnbull, my best friend and first horse show mentor; Wendy and Chelsea Wilkinson; Kathy and Hannah Botney; Harriet and Ali Berman; Susan, Cate, and Jenney Aselage; Kristi Shaw and Rachel Dede; Page and Sarah Tredennick; Elizabeth, Kelsey, and Sydney Glazer; Carlin Vickery and Julia Capalino; Alex Charters and Samantha Booth; Ann and Elsa Goding; Lisa and Anna Schierholz; Gary Kart and daughter Brittany; Terri Combs and Katie Swartwood; Charles, Marylynn, Jacque, and Sylvia Murray; Brian, Hannah, and Meredith McLean; Peter and Leney Roberts; and Tom, Lorraine, and Alex May.

I have met many trainers over the years who have inspired my respect and appreciation for their teaching and for their patience with my questions and also for their care and kindness to my daughter. To these people I express my deepest gratitude; Geoff Teall, Susan Baginski and Patty Boland, Melinda Antisdal and Sarah Jane Franklin, Val Lowe, Katana O'Brien, Jane Schwaggert, CeCe Bloum, Lori DeRosa and Erin Duffy, Pat Lautenbach and Gretchen Vosburgh, Janet Harms, and Juan Ledgard.

Introduction

If you are new to the horse show world, this book will serve as a map and guide to help you navigate around one of the sporting world's most unusual and idiosyncratic venues. If you and your child are already participating, this book will serve as a backup and hopefully provide some comic relief during those long days and head-scratching moments of confusion and frustration.

Most parents find themselves at horse shows or horse or dressage trials after their children have been riding for some time. This is not always the case, but this book proceeds on the assumption that your child already has a trainer and is at least contemplating showing. In that regard, the book discusses the suitability of your child's instructor as a horse show trainer, buying an appropriate show-quality horse or pony for your child, the show clothing and other necessary items, and what to expect at horse shows: winning and losing, judging, terminology, and horse showing as the Great Meaning of Life (oops, maybe not *that* far).

General chapters that apply to all Horse Show Moms are followed by those that are specific to your child's discipline. You can read some now or skip right to the disciplines for clues about the meaning of your particular show day. I've included information on types and levels of shows and their classes and divisions, and year-end and cumulative awards. However, in every case, you must hold your discipline's rule book as the final authority. While I've made every effort to ensure accuracy, rules change over the years; plus, the more you become familiar with the rule books, the more you can relax and enjoy yourself at the shows.

Dressage riders and eventers should please forgive me for using the generic term "horse show." I know full well that your competitions are called trials or events, but in my overview chapters, I have used the more generally recognized term for the sake of simplicity. Similarly, I will use "she" when referring to the rider throughout, with the understanding that horse show participants are predominantly female.

When reading this book, you will notice that some of what I've written is tongue-in-cheek, and some is written while *biting* my tongue. The horse show and event world can stir up some mighty passionate emotions. It's one thing to be told by your child's volunteer Little League coach to go sit in the bleachers, but quite another thing to hand over thousands of dollars to care for a live creature and *then* be told to go sit in the bleachers. I hope that what I've written here will provide some solace in the fact that there are plenty of Horse Show Moms and Dads out there feeling the same thing every rainy weekend in the mud. In any event, enjoy this book, enjoy your child, and enjoy the *ride!*

First Things First

What is a horse show? A horse show is a sporting event like no other. Even if you, as a Horse Show Mom, have been to one, you know that there are many ways to describe it. Its most useful purpose for your child is to test and solidify the skills she's been learning at the barn or at home. It also helps to strengthen the skills and training of her horse or pony. For you, it could be a test of your walking and running skills, your patience and waiting skills, your preparedness skills, and a test of your dignity, humor, and flexibility.

In some equestrian disciplines, and in most at the top levels, showing is the goal. All the lessons and training that go on at the barn have just one ultimate goal: the horse show. This means that the training is geared toward winning at the shows, and the horses bought and sold for your child and other customers at the barn are those that would do well at shows in the most efficient way possible. The horses are very well prepared before going to the show, and then prepped when they get there in such a way to guarantee the student achieves the most success possible.

For others, the horse show is just an occasional event that measures the success of at-home training. In this case, there are no goals for accumulation of points or winning, per se, other than the desire to see where the training has gone well, or what areas need more focus, or just to add a little fun and spice to the everyday routine.

Horse show ahead.

There are many different equestrian disciplines that compete in shows. Several have national awards, most have state and regional awards, and there are three that have Olympic teams: dressage, show jumping, and eventing. The latter three fall under the catch-all definition of "English" riding sport. Western riding, a huge competitive industry, has many different styles of competition, most famously the rodeo. Quickly coming up on the international horizon is reining, which in 2004 became an Olympic exhibition sport and may well become a regular event at the Olympics. In addition, there are other non-Olympic international competitions for vaulting, endurance riding, and driving.

This book will cover hunter/jumpers, dressage, eventing, and the Western breed shows. While all of these disciplines share the horse as the core component, each has its own approach, style, goals, and requirements for competing, both financial and otherwise. We, as horse show parents, all share some common ground. We have kids who ride, trainers who train them, horses and ponies that compete and take care of our kids (or not), and a host of items that need to be purchased for both the kids and their mounts. There are barns for board, venues for horse shows, judges, awards, ribbons, and trophies, goals to accomplish, feelings to be soothed, progress to be assessed, and sacrifices to be made by parents, siblings, *and* the rider. Welcome to the horse show world.

At some levels of competition, horse showing can be done on a very small budget. There are one-day shows where you can "jump out" and show for the day but keep your horse in your trailer (hence, the term "jump out") or tied up outside. Other horse shows require at least a weekend in a hotel for you, your child, and her trainer, plus trailering fees to the venue.

Whatever kind of showing you do, the first thing to understand is that it takes time. Showing up for your kid's horse show is not like showing up for a two-hour soccer match. Horse shows generally run all day, have many different divisions, and your child may show in one to several classes throughout the day, not usually consecutively, and usually not for more than five minutes at a time. What this means for you is that you will be there all day, and have the thrill of watching her compete in very short segments, and then wait around for the next class, repeat the process, and wait again.

Another aspect of showing which is very unlike soccer is that although your child and her horse are a team, this is not your normal team sport. This is not a sport that requires her to be just a good goalie while the others on her team can be good passers or play good defense. There is no yelling "Pass the ball!" or "C'mon, take a shot!" Instead, there are very particular non-verbal aids and cues that she gives to a very large animal several times her body weight. And for the most part, it works—miraculously. It can be a thrill and a wonder to watch. And then again, the sight can also be amazingly boring or disappointing—exhilarating or exhausting by turns. Your child might be having a good day, but her mount is in a slump. On other days, her horse is perfect, but your child is tired, or cranky, or just not *on*. And then there are those days when they are both at their peak and it never gets better than this, no matter what the level of competition. Riding a horse is one of the most intense multitasking sporting activities in the world, and when it all comes together, it is a particularly beautiful thing to watch.

There are all kinds of shows for each discipline, and each one has different levels of showing. (Note that eventers never refer to their competitions as "horse shows," but for simplicity's sake, all competitions will be referred to that way.)

Here is a general rundown of the types of shows you might attend with your child.

SCHOOLING SHOWS

Each discipline has this kind of entry-level show. Some have different names, but the purpose is the same. It is typically one day only, can be held either at a private barn or cross-country property, or at a regular arena. It may even be held at the barn where you board. It usually has the cheapest entry fees, the cheapest stall fees (and often, no stalls), and is a "non-rated" show, meaning that it carries no points for state, regional, or national year-end awards, nor are there classes that would be "qualifiers" for other events. (Exception: If a local barn runs a series of these schooling shows, there may be awards for the series. For example, if your child attended all of the shows in this series, she might qualify for a series award based on how she did in each particular show.)

The judging at these shows is often done by trainers or others not necessarily licensed to judge at "recognized" shows, usually picked for their willingness. Experience and fairness are pluses that encourage the exhibitors to come back.

The purpose of these shows is manyfold:

- To get young or green (meaning inexperienced) horses into the ring at a reasonable cost for the purpose of schooling the horse for its overall education and training.
- To get beginner students into the ring or on the field where the competition is easy and unintimidating. This is a great way to start a horse show experience. Because schooling shows are primarily small venues with fewer exhibitors (the "competitors," in horse show lingo), it is usually easy for your child to get a ribbon and thus be rewarded for her efforts in a tangible way, even if her skills are a bit raw. It can be a big confidence booster, allowing her to see what it is like to show and discover whether or not she really likes it. If she doesn't like it, you can stop right here and buy that vacation house!
- To have an inexpensive venue for exhibitors. While this may not be the goal of most horse show management, trainers with big barns or a decent facility will occasionally offer these shows to their own clients who cannot otherwise afford to show. They will also usually open these shows to other barns in the area as a means to boost the competition numbers and help defray the costs. They will often allow clients (young and old) who do not own their own horse to show a school horse (venues that are close to home are not as physically demanding on an older school horse as a rated show might be).
- To get ready for the showing season. A trainer may often take a group from her barn to a schooling show before the regular rated season (see next page) starts to get the adult clients, kids, and horses prepped for the coming competition. For a new trainer, it's a great way to test her own ability at schooling several students and finding out if she needs to bring along more help.

Requirements for Schooling Shows

- There are five basic elements to horse showing (apart from the financial): a mount (horse or pony), a rider, equipment, clothing, and transportation. You've got the rider, either you or your trainer will provide both the mount and/or the transportation, and the equipment will be the minimum safety and riding gear needed for your discipline. Fancy show clothes are usually unnecessary, although you wouldn't know this at some Western schooling shows. If the show is not at your barn, you will usually need to provide a negative Coggins certificate (see glossary), which provides proof that your horse does not have Equine Infectious Anemia (EIA). If you are traveling out of state, you may also need a health certificate from your vet stating that your horse is free from other infectious diseases.

RATED (OR RECOGNIZED) SHOWS OR EVENTS

Rated or "sanctioned" shows are those that are recognized as official shows by your discipline's organization. Each discipline has an organization that approves show venues, judges, and course designs. These organizations also make the rules, tally your child's points, and award year-end awards. These organizations are detailed in the chapters that cover each discipline, and for the English disciplines, the United States Equestrian Federation (USEF) is a main overseeing parent. (It also has its own Western component, but, as yet, most breed disciplines do not require dual membership in the USEF in order to compete in their shows.) Common to all showing is the fact that these shows are "rated," "recognized," or "sanctioned," as the discipline lingo may call them, and occasionally, some are rated higher than others. Essentially, this means that a higher-rated show carries more points for year-end awards, and therefore, the competition will usually be tougher.

The reasons for going to a rated show are as varied as the colors of horses and the disciplines that have shows. Showing allows your child (and her trainer) to gauge her progress with her horse; it also satisfies a deeper competitive drive than the non-rated shows. If you and your child get committed to her discipline and want to see her succeed in a big way, rated shows are a must.

For all shows and events—rated, non-rated, sanctioned, and non-sanctioned—you will need the following:

- A good sense of humor.
- Patience.
- Food (large horse show venues have food concessions, but you may find the fare expensive and not particularly nutritious).

- A book, the newspaper, needlework, or other boredom-quelling devices.
- Band-Aids, clean wipes, acetaminophen or ibuprofen, Kleenex.
- Comfortable clothes (for you)—nothing fancy; preferably those clothes you don't care about. One thing this is not, is a fashion show.
- Shoe polish and leather cleaner.
- If you're helping to groom your child's pony or horse: horse shampoo, brushes, curry comb and hoof pick, plus braiding supplies if needed.

For rated shows you will also need:
- the required riding clothing and tack;
- more money; and
- a bigger sense of humor.

You may need to stay more than one day; you may need the services of a groom (in some disciplines); you may need a professional braider; and

Needlepoint and empathy.

you may need to pay your trainer more money than you did for the schooling show. You could be held responsible for your trainer's lodging and meals, usually split among all the competitors that your trainer brings to the show. If you use a groom, you will need to pay the going groom's rate, and then also tip him or her. For some disciplines, your child's horse or pony will need to be body-clipped and have its mane pulled. Usually done before you leave for the show, this is one part of the expense.

When all tallied up, a horse show can cost anywhere from fifty dollars to a mind-blowing two thousand dollars-plus a weekend, particularly if you, your child, your trainer, and grooms have to stay in a hotel.

Are you running away yet? Don't. There are many ways that families can figure out how to help their horse-crazy kids get to horse shows and proudly demonstrate their growing expertise. Though there are parents who can easily afford to show year-round, there are many others who make choices about dinners out, vacations, or that new car. And most parents say they wouldn't trade any of it back. Seeing your child navigate a difficult course over jumps or performing complicated dressage patterns, watching her brave a cross-country ditch and water or sliding a reining horse to a perfect stop is uniquely thrilling in the "parent as spectator" sporting world. And don't forget the quieter thrill of watching perfectly appointed five-year-olds with their ponies in halter at a Western show.

You may have been caught unawares and unprepared for this life in the equestrian world, or you may be revisiting your own childhood experience. However you got here, if you bought this book, you're on the road to quite an experience.

CHAPTER

2

What to Expect

THE HORSE SHOW AS VENUE

Welcome to the horse show, the premier venue for mud, manure, bad food, cold, heat, rain, and sometimes snow. This may be the only event of your life where you will shell out hundreds of dollars for the privilege of standing around all day in the rain. For the uninitiated, getting used to the horse show world takes time (and sometimes, time and time again). It's a given that your senses and sensibilities will be overwhelmed as you look around for touchstones to your normal life. Horse shows are not created for their amenities. Many a new Horse Show Mom has said "I will never use a porta-potty!" God finds this amusing, of course, and shows us who is really in charge.

The "facilities."

"Never" soon becomes "only in emergencies," evolving to "just this once," to "just this weekend," to "I said *what?*" A few horse shows later that same mom is saying, "They have really nice porta-potties here."

But first, there is the pre-show packing. This can be a nice mother/daughter ritual, or a nerve-wracking nightmare. Staying organized between shows helps, as does having a checklist for everything you need to bring. Each discipline will have its own special requirements, so use the lists below as a basic guideline and customize them yourself.

What to Bring

This first list is for your child's tack trunk so she doesn't forget her essentials. The other list is for you.

RIDER'S TACK TRUNK
- Helmet
- Protective vest (for cross-country eventers)
- Gloves
- Whip, crop, and/or spurs if used
- Shoe polish
- A shoe sponge for last-minute touch-ups (cheaper at a discount store than at horse shows)
- Hair nets
- Towels and rags
- Sunscreen
- Band-Aids
- Tail wrap
- Extra snaps for buckets, halters, etc.
- Saddle pads or blankets
- Bell boots, jumping boots, or whatever your discipline requires
- Any pony/horse sheets or blankets necessary for protection from the weather or from flies
- Bottled water
- Some type of snack food, such as protein bars
- A grooming tote with:
  - Brushes
  - Hoof pick

- Shampoo and tail de-tangler
- Fly spray
- Braiding supplies if needed

Also, check off:

- Saddle
- Bridle and tack
- Boots
- Show clothes and jewelry (if part of your discipline)

Stuffed pockets.

MOM'S PACK

Most Horse Show Moms develop a good sense of what to have on hand, and everyone has her favorite way to haul it all around. Fanny packs are out of vogue, and no matter how useful they would be at horse shows, no one seems to be using them these days. My teenage daughter would die if I resorted to this useful item, so I've gotten into the habit of wearing only pants or shorts that have many deep pockets. In cold weather I fill up my sweatshirt or jacket pockets, too. I'm not sure walking around with numerous bulges (plus cameras over the shoulder) is any more chic than using a fanny pack, but the captain of our family's fashion police calls the orders on this one. (For those who throw caution to the wind, you could use a backpack or tote bag of some sort to carry these necessities.)

- Kleenex (multipurpose, but particularly for the lovely restrooms)
- Packaged hand wipes
- Band-Aids
- Tylenol or Advil
- Sunscreen
- 2 to 3 bobby pins
- A scrunchy hair thingy (for ponytails)
- A small needle and thread, plus at least one button
- Safety pins
- An aspirin or two for bee stings (Crush and wet to make a paste and spread over the sting. It soothes quickly.)
- A good sunhat (for yourself)
- Bottled water
- Boredom busters: needlework, crossword puzzles, the newspaper, a book
- No expectations

In your car, or some other handy place, have the following:
- Extra bottled water
- First-aid kit with antibacterial cream, anti-itch cream, Band-Aids, an ace bandage, an instant ice pack or two, tweezers

CLOTHING

One-day shows close to home will be the easiest to prepare for. You can tell what the weather is like, pack your own food, and bring along a thermos of coffee. Weekend "away" shows are not as easy. In the summer you will need plenty of sunscreen, water, a hat and rain gear for those unexpected downpours that didn't show up on your Yahoo! weather page. If you live or show anywhere north of the Mason-Dixon Line, fall and spring shows will require a more extensive wardrobe: warm-weather clothes for unexpectedly hot days, rain gear, polar fleece (and sometimes down) jackets. And if you have to begin your day before dawn, you may be wearing the entire gamut of your wardrobe all in one day.

Winter shows will generally be indoors, but don't count on being warm. Most indoor shows only have minimal heat in the barn area, sometimes none. Long underwear is a must, and you'll be grateful to have warm, woolly socks if you're standing around a lot. If you're sitting, bring something (folding bleacher seat, polar fleece, thick newspaper) to put between your seat and the possibly freezing-cold bleacher seats. Oh, and don't forget shoes: waterproof, manure-proof, and nonslippery in the mud. They should be comfortable, and ones you can run in—as in back to the barn or your car for whatever your child inevitably forgot.

Packing for the weekend.

The Day Begins

If you didn't start your day in the dark hitching up a horse trailer, you may be getting up at the crack of dawn after your less-than-restful night at the local Super 8 Motel. Your child's pony or horse may need a bath, a lunge (a run-around exercise spin on a long rope to get him calm enough for your child to ride), and definitely, some grooming. Your trainer may want your child to school in the ring or cross-country as early as you used to get up for her middle-of-the-night feedings. You may find yourself drinking coffee made with hose water and be grateful for the caffeine, no matter the form.

Now that you're up, you can begin to prepare for all the other things that may happen in your day. If your eventing child is doing a cross-country course, you may be asked to judge at one of the cross-country obstacles. If you're at a one-day show, you may be doing all the grooming either in your trailer or in your trainer's trailer. You may be asked to get breakfast or lunch for the whole group (you are a mom, after all), and you may be cleaning tack in between stall mucking, feeding, grooming, and squeezing in some time to watch your child's classes. And don't forget videotaping.

It may be up to you to get your child and her mount to the gate or starting box on time. If your trainer is running late at another ring, you may be negotiating with the gatekeeper for a later spot in the starting order for your child, or at least for patience until the trainer gets there. If you're at an event, and your child doesn't start her course on time, those minutes will be added to her course time. At a dressage show, she'll be eliminated if she misses her assigned time. All of this timing is crucial. It's up to your trainer to negotiate her conflicts with the different rings and students, but you may be called upon to help out. The gatekeepers of the world are used to this, and although some take delays in stride, others take it in pride—as in pride for keeping their gate running smoothly with no concern for *your* problem. Keen diplomatic skills will come in handy.

Dining

One of your main jobs will be negotiating the food maze. Some venues will have no food. Others will have a small stand selling fast food, so if eating an occasional dry hamburger on a stale bun doesn't offend your palate, you'll be fine. But for those with more persnickety tastes, you'll have to assume palatable food to be one of your bigger challenges. Anyone can pack enough food for a one-day show, even given the predawn alarm, but if you're going to be at the show all day, each day, and for an entire weekend, you'll need to scope out what's available at the show or nearby.

"Nearby" is a relative term at horse shows. It may mean across the road or it may mean ten miles down the road. Open countryside suitable for most horse shows is not usually convenient to Pizza Hut. Larger horse show venues will have better food choices, but then you may find yourself paying exorbitant amounts for the privilege of buying a salad prepared right before your eyes: one poured out of a bag into a Styrofoam box, and that will be eight dollars, please. Oh, and don't forget the tip jar.

So if you're not prepared, you may have to either go hungry, or eat a few meals that are not on your diet, or that you may not recognize as food.

Ala carte (before the horse) menu.

———————————   U   ———————————

The Horse Show Mom: In my nine years as a Horse Show Mom, I've had more than a few food adventures. As a quasi-vegetarian committed to feeding my family healthy organic meals, it's been one of the bigger boundary breakers of my Horse Show Mom's experience to have to make do on horse show fare. Don't get me wrong. Horse show food is no worse than food at any other sporting event, a fact that in itself has always been a major head-scratcher for me. Why do sporting events have the worst food? What about the scientifically supported notion that athletic performance is related to diet? What about the popular media telling us "we are what we eat"? And in this sport, which is not football, no serious equestrian is trying to go for the body built by Hungry Man dinners.

A few years ago we started going to a new indoor showing venue in the Midwest. I was really happy to see garden burgers on the menu at the snack bar. However, they forever remained "virtual" garden burgers, as the snack bar never got them in. I think they wanted to see how much interest there would be before they actually went out and bought them. Unfortunately, I may have been the only one to ask for them. On another occasion I asked for the egg and muffin special, only to be told that they didn't have the "right" kind of eggs to make those. I am still at a loss on that one. We immediately nicknamed the snack bar the "Twilight Zone Eatery," and it remains so to this day.

Networking with other parents is helpful in finding decent (or any) local restaurants. Often a grocery store is just as good for finding premade deli food to take out. And "take-out" is what you'll need, because if you dawdle, you may miss that two-minute round that you drove two hundred miles and waited all day to see.

If you are going to be at a show for an entire weekend and are concerned about the meal choices, here are a few ideas for healthy things to bring along that will at least keep the hunger at bay until the evening, when you can relax at a restaurant. (Note: A medium-size canvas cooler is flexible for a variety of items but still strong enough to keep all the sniffing dogs away.)

- Fruit, both fresh and dried
- Bags of nuts
- Canned tuna or salmon (don't forget a can opener and forks)
- String cheese (will keep for the weekend in its wrappers)
- Juice boxes
- Fruit leathers
- Protein bars

———————————— U ————————————

The Horse Show Mom: I have a favorite little recipe given to me by my friend, Toby Lieb, for some protein-rich dried fruit and nut "cookies." They are sweet, but have no sugar, and they are packed with protein. They can be made up to a week before the horse show and stored in baggies or an airtight container.

> ### Dried Fruit Cookies
>
> Take equal amounts of your favorite nuts and dried fruits (I use cashews, almonds, dates, dried apricots, and whatever else happens to be in the kitchen at the time). Soak overnight with enough water to cover them. Drain and blend all ingredients together in a blender until smooth. Spoon onto lightly greased cookie sheets, press flat with the back of the spoon, and bake in the oven on its lowest setting for a few hours until they are slightly firm throughout.

MOM'S (AND DAD'S) ROLE AT THE SHOW

Parental roles can be an area of great confusion, controversy, and stress, but they don't have to be. Different disciplines have different needs, but mostly it's up to three people: you, your child, and the trainer. Most trainers have a specific way of doing things, and while yours should let you know what she expects from you and your child at a horse show, this little piece of information often falls into the "assumed" file. That is, the trainer assumes that you'll know how she wants things done. Some trainers love to have all the help they can get, but never at the ring. Other trainers will leave you to negotiate her lateness with the gatekeepers, while still others will love for you to apply that last-minute shine on your child's boots. You are better off clearing this matter up at the beginning; if your trainer tells you to "go sit in the stands" in front of everybody, you will feel like a very clueless horse show parent.

If you are helping with the grooming, you will be busy indeed, in addition to your maternal role. This is an important job, and you need to have some skills. Your child may be doing her own grooming at home and at the barn, but perhaps she needs your help at the horse show. In order to avoid a complete breakdown of your finely tuned parent/child roles, it's best to learn the skills before undertaking the grooming responsibility at a show. Plan ahead and take some lessons either from your child or another experienced horse show parent. Knowing what to expect ahead of time and knowing your trainer's standards are the key to a smooth-running show experience.

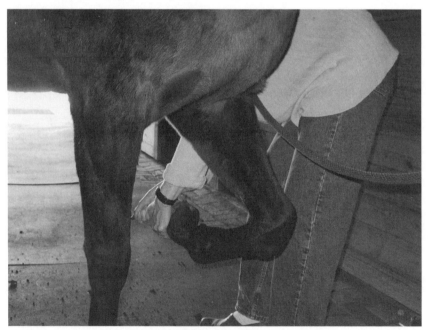

Picking hooves.

―――――――――― U ――――――――――

The Horse Show Mom: In our first couple of years of showing, our small barn traveled to shows without grooms. Most of the girls— teenagers with one horse each—managed everything themselves. Because my daughter Chétie was only seven years old when we started, I was her groom, stall mucker, and mom, all at once. Our trainer had high standards for grooming, having worked for a large show barn during college. I would regularly get sent back to the wet stall with that blue whitening shampoo to get Dewey, our white pony, ever whiter. My most vivid memory is of a gray and freezing November morning at six A.M., feeling the shock of ice water as it made its way under the cuff of my down jacket, all the way up my arm and down my back. And that was only my first chore of the day.

Chétie was always there "helping" as only young children can: combing Dewey's tail over and over, feeding carrots and treats, and picking hooves (her favorite chore). For me, there remained stall mucking, unbraiding, cleaning off those lovely green spots that Dewey would invariably get as he rolled in his muck throughout the day, cleaning tack, tacking up, polishing boots . . . and the list went on. When our barn finally got some grooming help, I was first in line with the cash. At least, that is, until Chétie was old enough to put a competent dent in the chores.

If you are showing with a big show barn, grooms will most likely do all the horse work, and your trainer may want you to remain quietly in the background. For others, invisible is better. Every trainer has his or her own preference. If you like to be involved and help, ask your trainer what you can specifically do to help the day go more smoothly for all concerned.

One thing you will most definitely be responsible for is paying your show bills. Often, your child will not be able to get her competitor's number until you've made an initial visit to the show office with that check or credit card. At the end of the show, checking out is mandatory, and while in some cases the trainer will do so, or appoint someone to do it, it's usually the banker (you) who gets to do the job. The office is often a great place to see other parents parting with their own hard-earned cash, giving you an ideal opportunity to commiserate.

If your barn does have grooming help, you need to have cash for tips. Every barn handles this matter in a different way, so ask ahead of time to avoid adding an ATM run to all of your other responsibilities as you get ready to head home.

THE END OF THE DAY

The last hours of a show can find you exhausted and cranky, particularly when you realize that going home can be at least as much work as getting there. You're not as rested, and your child is tired, too. Even if she's going home with ribbons, the adrenaline letdown for both of you is significant enough to make the ride home a bad-tempered affair even for the mellowest of souls. Getting packed to go home is never as exciting as packing to go to the show, and often little Miss Blue Ribbon is off chatting with friends or packing her trunk so slowly that you may find yourself counting to ten over and over to keep your tired sense of patience aloft. In addition, she never got her homework done.

What am I doing? you may ask. Well, you're doing your best at being a Horse Show Mom, which will mean nothing to her teachers, not much to your husband (unless you're the dad, of course), and your friends already think you're crazy. But in those long stretches of grumpy silences, there will be a priceless moment or two, in between the panicked "Did you bring your saddle?!" and "Where are your new boots?" when you and your child share a remembrance or salient observation of the weekend. And this precious little fragment of conversation, or that smile or laugh will be what she remembers twenty years from now. Old and decaying ribbons in a plastic box will not hold a candle to the significance of your closeness, and the memory of all that hard work you did just for her.

The Barn Universe

The barn is your horse's home. It's where he lives with other horses, sleeps, gets turned out in a paddock or pasture (or not), is ridden, and fed. It is of primary importance that your horse is happy, safe, clean, and well nourished. You and your child's relationship with her horse or pony (or both) cannot be forged in the best possible way if your horse's basic needs are not met. And while you may have been boarding at your barn for some time and are quite happy with the arrangement, look around as if you are seeing it with new eyes, and go down this list of questions as if you were searching for a home for a new horse.

- Is what you see what your horse needs? That is, CTC—which stands for Clean stalls, Turnout, Company of other horses.
- Is the barn clean?
- Are the aisles free from clutter and machinery? This is for everyone's safety, including your child's.
- What kind of turnout schedule is there? Turnout is the horse's grazing time in the pasture or paddock. Grass is the best, but what is available in one part of the country may not be available where you live. Horses in some parts of the country become quite accustomed to turnout in a dirt or sand paddock. At the least, there should be some type of a rotating schedule that keeps your horse happily grazing or getting fresh air for part of every day.

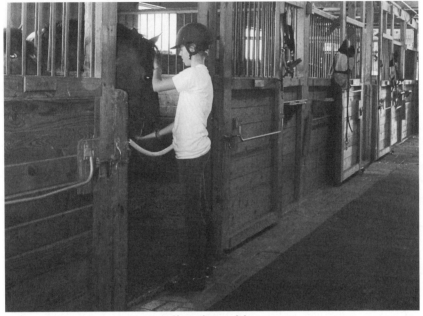

Clean barn aisle.

- Are the stalls mucked regularly? Once a day would be a minimum to give your horse a clean space to lie down on, as well as to keep down the number of flies. Twice a day would be better.
- Are stalls free from nails, are they properly bedded, and do they have grills or windows so the horse can look out at the rest of his world?
- Is hay offered throughout the day?
- Is there plenty of water in every bucket? Hydration is very important for horses, and a horse should always have fresh water available.
- How often is the water changed? Twice a day is ideal, but at the minimum the water should be clean, free from algae, and palatable. Water is even more important than a clean stall.
- Where is the manure pile in relation to the barn? It should be far enough away to minimize flies, and spread daily or removed on a regular basis.
- Are the horses plagued by flies, and if so, what's being done about it? Automatic fly sprayers are great, in addition to other efforts to keep all insects from breeding.

- Is there someone on the premises at all times? If not, what happens in case of a fire or tornado?
- Where is the feed kept? Preferably in airtight bins.
- What is the standard for feed? Does your barn provide grain appropriate to your horse's needs and fitness level? Is the feed adjusted for changes in routine? Can you request a specific feed?

You may be saying *"Whoa!* This is more responsibility than I care to have. I don't know anything about feed!" True, you may not. However, sometime in your child's riding career, you may have a horse that loses weight, grows too fat, or develops a strange malady that will require special attention. What you want to know here is if that attention will be easy or hard to get at your barn. It is not always the case that a little bit of knowledge is dangerous (though a lot of knowledge is always better than some, some is always better than none). Trainers may come and go at your barn, and the care may change with rotating stable help. Keeping an eye on your horse's environment helps the horse, your child, and your investment. And while your trainer may be very capable of handling all situations, the best relationships with horses come from knowing about them— the ideal way for your child to learn responsibility and become a capable rider at the same time.

U

The Horse Show Mom: I would not consider myself to be an expert in equine nutrition. However, a couple of years ago we brought Petey, our young Irish Sport horse, to the barn where we have always boarded our horses. Our trainer had moved away, and the barn had been taken over by a wonderful lady who loves horses in every way, but neither she nor I had experience with a fresh six-year-old jumper. It took some experimenting between us and lots of advice from other friends and trainers to hit upon a perfect balance of what amount of grain (and of which type) and how many hours of grass turnout would keep weight on him, as well as keep him from being too fresh for Chétie to ride.

PEOPLE SAFETY

Once you know your horse is happy and safe, check that the environment is also safe for your child.

- Is an adult present at all times when children are riding?
- Is there an adult present—preferably your trainer—who is trained in Basic Life Support? Riding is a dangerous sport. After all, we're often talking about 80-pound children with 700-pound ponies, or even 1,200-plus-pound horses. Falls are the most dangerous, but accidents can happen even inside the barn. Basic Life Support is a four-hour class that is inexpensive and readily available. And while basic first aid may be all that is ever necessary, it's nice to know that your trainer or someone else at the barn cares enough about her charges to be prepared.
- Take a look at the first-aid kit. Is it new? If it's older, is it restocked regularly?
- Are emergency phone numbers for ambulance and hospitals displayed by the phone? Is there an emergency contact list of parents nearby? Be sure that you update this frequently with new work or cell phone numbers.
- Again, what is the plan in case of fire?

The Horse at Home

If your barn is at your home, you will either have a trainer visiting you, or you will be trailering to your trainer's barn. There are many advantages to having a horse at home. Your child's relationship with her horse is more primary: they see each other every day, and horse and child can bond in a more intimate way than in a boarding situation. (However, the responsibilities are greater, which may be a problem for a busy family.) Also be aware that if your child is involved in horse shows, your life will be very, *very* busy. Lessons will become more important, and as your child progresses, your trainer may want to be more involved in the everyday "at home" riding program. This will vary from discipline to discipline. Hunter/jumper and eventing trainers may not want your child to be jumping at home, particularly if no one else in the family rides. Jumping is like gymnastics: An experienced spotter on the ground is critical, as is having someone around in case of a fall. And for all the disciplines covered here, there will always be time in your child's or pony's career where they are at a juncture in their training program, when it's really important to have consistent and more frequent training.

YOUR BARN FAMILY

The other important aspect of the barn is your barn family: your trainer, the people who work at the barn, and the people and horses who board there. When we are looking for a trainer, it's often the trainer's qualities and competence that we focus on most. This is natural. If our child is to compete and grow in the sport, we want the best instruction that is available. Sometimes the best we can get means the only thing available; other times it means the best that's within a comfortable driving distance. Often it's the best we can afford. But no matter what, the trainer comes with a barn family, something to be considered.

Horse showing is a sport that involves a lot of time away from home, and that time away from home is spent with a "family." Unlike other sports, it's not a "team" of kids with one trainer, such as soccer, basketball, or tennis, but a family of many different characters, ages, genders, and walks of life. Also unlike other sports, the group is not necessarily a team. At large barns, several kids very often compete against each other in the same division. Even though the trainer's goal may be for all of the kids to do well, there is bound to be competition at home as well.

The amount of time your child spends with the barn family is significant enough to influence her feeling of well-being and challenging enough, even in the best-case scenarios, to be important for your consideration. This is not to say that you should be picky and overprotective. Every environment is a learning environment and allows a child to hone good social skills for her future as a grown-up. However, you want to be sure that the skills she's learning are the ones you want her to learn, are appropriate for her age level, and in line with your parenting goals.

Friends relaxing at the show.

For example: If you have an eight-year-old daughter and there are only teenage children around, you will want to be sure that they are kind to her, not constantly talking about their latest love conquests, and that they serve as reasonably good role models in the care of their horses, the language they speak, and in life in general.

You don't have to be obsessive, but be aware that although your trainer is not a babysitter, your child will be spending as much time at the barn as she might be at a babysitter's, school, or day-care center, and these are areas where parents usually are obsessive about the environment.

Notice how the other kids—and adults—treat the barn help. Mucking stalls and taking care of horses is a back-breaking and sometimes dangerous job. The people who care for your horse should at least be treated with respect and with fondness if they are doing a great job with your horse. The old parenting adage "Do as I say, not as I do" has never worked, and it never will. Kids learn from watching, first and foremost, so if the barn culture is one of condescension, ridicule, and rudeness, that is how your child will learn to relate to those people in the world whom we would have a hard time living without. But if the people in the barn are thoughtful, courteous and respectful, your child will receive the bonus of learning very valuable life lessons completely unrelated to riding.

MONEY VS. LOTS OF MONEY VS. OUTRAGEOUS MONEY

Okay, now to the important stuff, a topic that is touchy and may offend some. Having show horse(s) costs money. Lots of it. It can be done on a shoestring, but rarely is. Competing is expensive. Period. Though some disciplines are much cheaper than others, money remains a relevant issue for everyone. An important fact to consider is that there will always be someone in your barn who has more money than you do. And most likely there will always be someone who has less than you. Some people who have lots of money will spend it carefully on one horse and go to few shows. Others with a strictly middle-class income will hock everything they have for their child's show career. And those who have outrageous money can and do buy the most expensive mounts (and often, several of them) for their child.

What does this do to the dynamics in your barn? It can be compared to having several families living under one roof trying not to be jealous over brother number one's new Porsche (the one that cost as much as brother number two's yearly income). Now, if you are the brother with the Porsche,

Porsche and Porschette.

you may be saying to yourself, Tough luck; I work seventy hours a week, I earned it. Nonetheless, it will affect the way you are treated by the rest of the family. If your family loves you, they may be momentarily jealous, but in general they will be rooting for you and wishing you well, and will only revisit that momentary jealousy on bad days. But if your family doesn't love you, they will be watching out for your tumble. You will also be the constant topic at family gatherings, and you can bet that your ears will be burning. So, the basic rule is this: You can have a lot of possessions if you're loved, and people won't mind so much. This love is earned by your attitude toward others. If you're arrogant or rude, every possession you have will be your undoing in the eyes of others.

Translated into barn politics, your barn family will be made up of grown-ups and kids from different income levels, middle income to millionaires, and sometimes, millionaires to billionaires. In addition, parents will have different parenting styles and different goals for their kids. With some it will be all about the schools they attend and the grades that they get; with others it will be more about the victory in the show ring. Some might have to spend a fortune on a pony to feel they are in the "club," and for others it will be more about the child's relationship with the horse. The barn is a microcosm of the world in which they will grow up, and while this is an important learning experience, the amount of money at stake can be inappropriate information for anyone under twenty-one. It is always surprising to find out how much the little tykes know about the price someone paid for a horse or pony, custom boots, saddle, or even the tuition at private schools. Big, big ears, uncanny telepathy, and sponge-like brains see all, hear all, and repeat it forever to their friends, then in the car during car pool, then at the dinner table at home, which then prompts any self-respecting horse show mom to start the cycle all over again.

The question is: Is the barn culture one where your child can make friends, enjoy the competition, and enjoy her horse? Can she feel that she can make progress on the best mount you can buy (or lease), and can she maintain self-respect in the face of losing to other, more expensively mounted barn companions? Equally as important, can you be happy in this barn for the amount of time you will spend there, and at the horse shows with the other parents? These things will be apparent to you now in your current barn situation. But when shopping for a new trainer or barn, it may take a while to get a feeling for the barn culture, so it's a good idea to interview the trainer, and if possible, board your child's horse or pony there for a week or two on a trial basis. Hang around with your child and see how she interacts with others. Whether the parents are friendly to you is also a good indicator of how the kids will be to her.

U

The Horse Show Mom: When my daughter, Chétie, started riding at age six, the other girls in the barn were eleven and twelve. The rest of the small barn was occupied by adults. Because she was small for her age and no competition for the other girls, Chétie quickly became everyone's mascot. The girls helped her with her pony, treated her well, and tried hard to make it to the short stirrup/pony ring whenever she was showing. She idolized these girls, and I'm happy to say that they lived up to that. I didn't have to censor their conversations, even as they got older and had more diverse social lives and experiences. Occasionally, when we would all be away together at a show, Chétie would be left behind due to the age difference and the closeness the older girls naturally shared. And although Chétie would sometimes be a little upset, I was always grateful for the kindnesses the girls did show her. As these girls grew up and moved on, Chétie and I both missed them dearly.

SHOW SCHEDULE

Another important point in a show barn is how often you can go to shows. If your budget only allows two shows per year, and 80 percent of the barn is on the road every month, your child may not be a match for this barn. In addition to feeling left out, she may not receive the most consistent training if the trainer is on the road all the time. This is usually more of a problem in small barns. Very large barns with forty-plus horses usually have a tiered schooling program that allows uninterrupted training at home. The plus here is that your child may be getting lessons from a few different

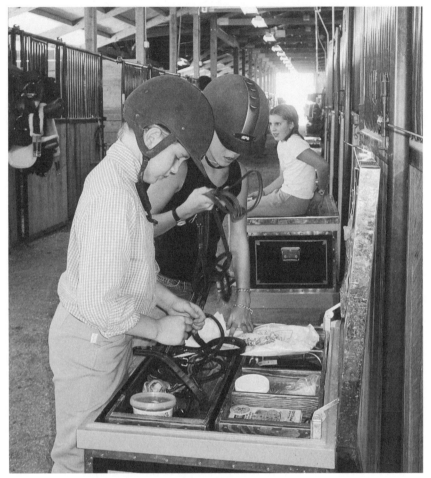

Sisters Kelsey and Sydney Glazer sharing a tack trunk.

teachers, and while they may not all be of the same caliber as the head trainer, an occasional change in perspective is good. Still, examine how your budget fits into the program for your barn. It may be better to forgo this level of training if it means constant heartache for your child because she's not on the road with the rest of the kids.

STAR STUDENTS VS. AVERAGE JOSEPHINAS

Riding is a sport with such broad appeal that it attracts not only people of all ages and incomes; it also attracts people of varying degrees of talent. Fortunately, there is room for everyone, because within the sport, the most hardworking and determined students often excel over those with greater athletic ability (and less work ethic). Many great riders, even Olympians, have successfully overcome body-type deficiencies and lack of natural ability to get to the top. They have done so with grit, determination, and a desire to win.

In a barn of several competing junior riders, some will always be better than others. There are those who arrive at their level of competition quickly and easily due to their natural ability and easy affinity with the horse, and others who are struggling to attain that level before their junior years run out. Most trainers will try hard to let the oldest kids get the most out of their final year, no matter what the ability. Others will focus more on the fourteen-year-old of unusual talent, which may be hard if your child is a senior and feeling left behind in her last year. A talk with your trainer about how it's making your child feel will help, as well as making a plan with your trainer for which shows your child can compete in to best highlight her abilities and reward her with the most success.

Not discounting the financial commitment, not every child is suited to national competition, and there are plenty of venues where a less talented or older beginner child can reap the same pleasures of ribbons and trophies that more capable students aspire to on a national level. Another point to remember is that at that national level, out of hundreds of kids competing, only a few win the year-end prizes. A child who wins regularly at local and regional shows may go off to college with fonder memories of success.

MOM'S (AND DAD'S) ROLE

What is your role here? Will you be spending as much time at the barn as your child does? Often when kids are young or just beginning, moms (or dads) will hang around and help with the grooming and tacking up. This may be your exact cup of tea, or the dishwater in your life you'd like to flush down the drain. Horses are not everyone's favorite Darjeeling. And even for the horsiest parents, to find this much time in their day can be, well, let's say impossible? How much you participate will be partially up to you, partially

Mucking the stall.

up to your trainer, and possibly have something to do with your pocket-book. Some barns may provide a grooming service ($$$), while others have older kids help out. Some trainers are very good about teaching your child good basic care of her horse and like to personally oversee this. Others will want to train you, the parent, so you can be responsible for having the pony ready on time.

In addition, there are lessons to watch, un-tacking, bathing, and finally, coaching your pony-loving kid back to the car. Whew! Who knew?

Lessons can be fun to watch, although in the beginning there may not be much to see as your child learns the basics. There is only so much some parents can take of watching their child go round and round at the walk and trot as she develops the necessary basic multitasking skills of hand, seat, and leg coordination, before she progresses to something more exciting. If she is having group lessons, you can have some fun with the other moms and dads by swapping stories and anxieties. Other parents are a great re-source for information, particularly if they've been at it a while. As time goes on and your child becomes more independent, hanging around the barn with her may not be as important or as necessary, or your child may want this time to herself and her barn friends. If you're busy and this suits you, great. If you want to be there, and you are feeling pushed out, set up a schedule with your child that allows both time for you to be there and also gives her some independent time.

BABYSITTER?

Another aspect of this barn dynamic is the combination of parents with different interests. For every barn full of dedicated Horse Show Moms, there are always several who would rather do anything but spend a day at the horse show. We all know these moms, and sooner or later we will be asked to take their child along with ours to the horse show. This is periodically a fun thing to do. It can be like a big summer sleepover, except that the kids know they have to get up early the next day and they're too tired from riding to resist an early bedtime.

Having a friend along with your child can quell some serious boredom if you're traveling in the car for hours, and can also make the whole event seem more like play than competition. Doing this favor for a friend who will reciprocate is one thing—doing it more than once for a less-involved and less-interested parent is another. The most valuable part of taking your child to shows is the one-on-one quality time that you get to spend with her. Giving that up will make you resent the other mom, the kid, and may also take some pleasure out of your days at the barn, particularly if you are worried about being pressured. So learn to say "no" and be happy with it. Remember that you signed on to parent only your own kids.

Overall, a barn culture can be a wonderful thing. In a large barn there are people of all ages and a variety of income levels who have horses for many different reasons: some to compete, some because horses have been a part of their lives from childhood, others to try to maintain (or regain) a sense of balance after a long week of intense work and commuting. These horsey people can all have a wonderful influence on your child, providing wisdom, insight, and comfort when things go wrong. The barn home can

The barn family of Maffit Lake Farm, Cumming, Iowa (photo courtesy of Richard Hildreth).

be filled with wonderful smells, friendly dogs and cats, horses and ponies of all sizes, and people of all generations. Members of your adopted barn family may over time become deeply cherished friends, and the relationships that you and your child develop will last well beyond your child's riding career. And the memories, of course, will last a lifetime.

The Trainer

No matter what the discipline, if your child competes, your child's trainer will become a very important part of your life. The trainer is the person responsible for giving your child the skills to relate to her horse, take care of her horse, ride the horse, and compete to the best of her ability. You need to have trust that the trainer is doing her job and that your child is progressing at a reasonable rate. You also need to have comfortable communication with your trainer so that you don't feel intimidated about asking questions, and if problems come up at the barn, you need an easy avenue for discussion.

All of this may seem elementary, but with people and relationships it is rarely as simple as it should be. People become trainers for a variety of reasons. Some are experienced and successful riders who train as a sideline to keep a riding career going. Some have retired from the ring but desire to continue in a sport that defines their life. Some are mediocre riders and fabulous teachers. Some are mean and grumpy to humans and kind and gentle to horses, while others are the exact opposite. Some are masters at what they do, while others are not; and many are capable and dedicated to both their students and their animals, no matter where they weigh in on the skill scale.

An excellent trainer knows that she needs to be part teacher, part psychologist, part business person, and part mentor. She must relate to her students and their paying parents in a professional and friendly manner. She

Kendall Bate and trainer Geoff Teall in an after-round conference (photo courtesy of Johnna Bate).

needs to be correct and timely about billing, honest and open about the child's ability and progress, and always an advocate for the student when purchasing a horse. This is a tall order in an industry that gave rise to the derogatory expression "horse trader," where commissions are earned on both ends of a sale (often with several hands passing through a purchase), and where good sense, safety, and basic horse care often take a backseat to competition.

THE BASICS

If you bought this book, you probably already have a trainer. You may be happy with the way things are going; you may want to tweak the situation a little; or you may be ready to flee. In any event, there are basic things your trainer should do for you and your child:

Show up on time for lessons. This is the most basic courtesy any business professional should provide. Although stable time is usually a little more inexact than office time, regular tardiness shows a lack of respect for *your* time, and will teach your child some unwanted habits. However, you must also be a flexible customer, allowing for emergencies, horse crises, people crises, etc.

Be clear about the billing. Right up front you need to know any charges that may be coming your way. One of the best things a trainer can do is have a printed brochure with services and prices. This is the twenty-first century after all, and it's not likely that your trainer doesn't own a computer and printer. If not, Kinko's and its photocopying offspring are in nearly every town in America.

Often trainers will have individual prices for single lessons and a discounted rate for a monthly program. For example, a "program" may include either four lessons or four rides per week. That way, if a child is going to miss a lesson, her horse or pony stays in work. Trainers usually charge less for group lessons, more for private.

Have a reasonable billing cycle. It can be enormously frustrating to never know when the bills are coming. The longer the billing cycle, the harder it will be for you to remember exactly how many lessons your child took or how many days of care at the show you are paying for. And while you and your trainer may have a good tracking system, there will be fewer questions in your mind if the bills are current. Trainers are busy people, working long hours and many continuous days (particularly when on the road at horse shows), and it's easy to let billing fall behind—but the foundation for all good business relationships is based on sound business practices.

Guidelines for buying tack and clothing. It's an expensive mistake to show up with new clothing or—even worse—new tack that your trainer doesn't like. Trainers should make this clear at the outset to save you money and frustration.

Communicate openly with you about your child's progress. This is not something that needs to be micromanaged. Learning to ride a horse in any discipline takes time, the best foundations being built slowly and with care, but your trainer should always make time for you, either informally or on a scheduled basis.

Help you understand your child's discipline. There is nothing more frustrating for a parent than being completely in the dark about what her child is doing, and paying a king's ransom for that privilege. You should be able to have your questions answered.

Have a fair and honest horse-buying policy. This topic is covered in more depth in Chapter 5, but your trainer should have a published list of fees involved in purchasing a horse. The list should include percentage of sale charged, suggested vetting and associated fees, what happens if the horse doesn't work out, and what fees will be charged when you sell your horse or pony.

Have a plan for when she is away at shows. This is difficult for the small barn with only one trainer. If the trainer has several students left behind while she attends shows with other riders, she needs to rethink her approach. She should either allow the other students to bring in another trainer while she is gone, or better yet, arrange for it herself. It's unfair to students who can't afford to show to be tied to a trainer that is frequently away. If it's only a few shows a year, then it's not a problem; some students might go to one or two fall or spring shows and others to a few in the summer. This arrangement can work if the trainer is sensitive to the needs of those left behind. But if the trainer has students at home while she is constantly on the road, she needs to make other arrangements. In larger barns that can support two trainers, one should always stay behind for the at-home clients.

YOUR SIDE

Aside from what you should expect from your trainer, there are a few ground rules that you as a parent should follow:

Be on time. A courtesy expected of one party should always be observed by the other. Getting ready for a lesson takes time, so always err on the high side. You and your child may be able to get ready in twenty minutes, so allow thirty at the minimum. Everyone is familiar with those days when you show up at the barn and your pony is either in the field playing hard to get, or your child's friend wants to chat about her recent adventure to Disneyland. Twenty minutes won't cut it, and your child may have to join a group lesson in progress, not be properly warmed up, and/or suffer the embarrassment and pain of the trainer's annoyance, or her wrath. If your child is a dawdler or needs to visit every pony in the barn before she tacks up, allow an hour. It will cut down on your stress and hers if you don't have to constantly whine and harangue her to hurry up.

Have your child outfitted properly. An approved helmet is a given, but is never useful if left at home. The same goes for socks, boots, chaps, vest (if worn), and adequate gear for inclement outings. Whatever your trainer wants your child to wear should be ready, clean, and on before she tacks up.

Do not interrupt your child's lesson. If you have questions, save them for the end or make an appointment with the trainer for another time.

Pay your bills on time. Your child needs to have your trainer's attention on the riding, not on when (or if) she will get paid.

BEYOND THE BASICS

There are many other ways a trainer can enhance business, customer relations, and your child's success. Although this book is not a training manual for trainers, a wish list is always a good thing to have in mind. Here's how trainers can graduate from goodness to greatness.

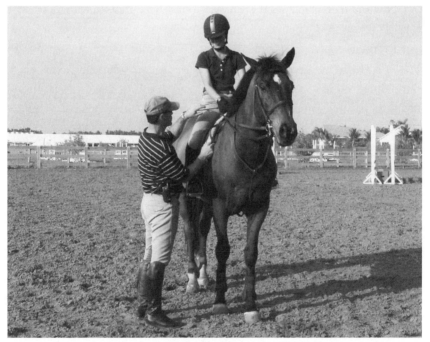

Lesson time with Olympic show jumper Peter Leone.

Show respect for you and your child. An experienced professional will know that even beginning students and parents with little knowledge for the sport or those with a tighter budget still need to be treated with respect for their interest and the commitment they are making. No one ever knows for sure who will eventually turn into a fabulous, award-winning student. In addition, how the trainer treats her less-important students is an indication of how she conducts her business in general.

Be a good role model. Children naturally look up to their teachers, parents, and caregivers. These are powerful roles that we all play, and children are the keenest observers on the planet. Everything your child's trainer does is up for close scrutiny. The manner in which the trainer addresses you, your child, other parents and students, the help, and other professionals in her field—all is closely observed and stored in the one million-gigabyte brains of six-year-olds. And while any trainer (or parent, for that matter) would be hard-pressed to survive such scrutiny, the most important point is that the trainer behaves in a professional and courteous manner while your child is in her company.

Have a mission. Good businesses often have mission statements; the best *always* do. It defines the company's philosophy and serves as a guideline for the company's outlook and goals. If a trainer defines her mission to herself and her customers, there will always be an assessment going on in the trainer's mind as to whether or not she's reaching her goals. It means, in short, that the trainer is taking her role seriously, her profession is meaningful in her life, and her success is important.

Stay abreast of the times. There are always new and innovative ways of doing things in the horse world. Sometimes it's a fad, sometimes it's ridiculous, sometimes it's just old things revisited (and for good reason), and sometimes it makes a lot of sense to everybody. Alternative therapies took a long time to catch on, but now they're basically mainstream. John Lyons, Pat Parelli, Buck Brannaman, Monty Roberts, and other "natural horsemanship" trainers have changed the way people think about and deal with horses, but they were all lone innovators in their time. It's in your trainer's best interest to be open-minded and investigate what's out there with regard to horse care, training, and nutrition. Nobody ever knows everything.

And it's often the more inexperienced trainer who is reluctant to try something new if it hasn't yet caught the fire of popularity.

Encourage students to attend clinics. Clinics—or group lessons—given by experts outside your barn are great opportunities to learn new approaches to old problems, hone in on little style nuances, and witness a master assessing a rider's progress and talent. There is nothing like hearing the same information from a fresh point of view. And while one might think that sending students to a clinic is a "no-brainer," some trainers are reluctant, for a variety of reasons, to expose their students to another trainer's style and expertise. Reasons include fear that students will want to leave the barn for the other trainer; fear that their students will be an embarrassment to them (this happens); or, the trainer thinks she knows it all—in which case, you're in trouble.

U

The Horse Show Mom: When a young rider grows sufficiently in maturity and skill to take clinics or lessons from the masters in her discipline, the relationship with these experts is often different from the trainer/rider relationship at home. Clinic time is tightly scheduled, and most of those giving master classes feel that the information they have to impart is important enough to expect the students to come prepared: well groomed and dressed (both horse and rider), and ready to ride (which means fit, hydrated, and not fainting from hunger). By the time your child reaches this point in her development she should have the discipline and prudence to be prepared for this kind of training. Having said that, any clinician who works students for hours in the hot sun without a water break is irresponsible and cruel to both horse and rider.

Attend clinics herself. Whether your trainer is young (or not) and still riding, either showing professionally or just training horses at home, she should still be taking help and advice from others. Any true master, whether athlete or artist, is constantly honing his or her skills. If your trainer is Olympic level, this, of course, is not as necessary as it is for the younger, less experienced trainer. But even the best international riders seek help from time to time from other masters in their field. If your trainer is no longer riding, she should be honing her teaching craft and keeping abreast of changes that may be happening in your discipline.

Be an advocate for her students. This means putting the student's (in this case, your child's) interests above those of her own—or yours for that matter—or other students in the barn, when there is an issue for your child alone. Which shows your child attends, the classes she enters, and whom she competes against should all be assessed by her trainer with an eye for what is in the best interest of your child as a student and developing rider. This attitude also means that when they are at the show, your trainer should show up to your child's ring on time, walk her course with her when appropriate, make sure that she is entering classes suitable for her skill level and her pony/horse's skill level, and that she is safe at all times. The trainer should be keenly aware of how fit her horses are, when they've been fed, and how much water they've had. The same should go for the students. It may be your job as a parent to see that your child is well hydrated, particularly on very hot days when there is a lot of standing around, but in your absence, this should also be on your trainer's radar. Trainers and coaches in all other athletic disciplines accept this responsibility. It has to do with fitness and peak performance, but often in the horse world, it is mostly the horses that are asked to be fit, not the students. Any world-class rider will say that their own fitness is a key component to their competitive abilities.

Have classroom sessions. There is so much to learn about horses and horsemanship. The United States Pony Club teaches this in a systematic way so that members can learn all aspects of horse care (and are actually required to demonstrate their knowledge in order to advance). This is often not the case in barns with professional trainers and very rarely outside the three-day eventing discipline. So much knowledge comes out on a "need-to-know" basis that one would think learning about horses requires some type of security clearance. And while it's understandable that little tykes need to learn to post before they can canter, and jog before they can

Classroom session.

lope, a simple lesson on the dangers of laminitis for treat-bearing pony owners (one cause of the ailment is overfeeding) is not a bad thing. Classroom sessions are a great rainy-day fill-in when the students can't ride, while monthly informative sessions for parents would save so much lesson and show-ring time, it's surprising that it's not an industry standard.

Have respect for your wallet. Riding and showing is a very expensive sport, and the money that pays for it comes from your hard work and dedication to your child. But for some reason, the horse industry may stand on its own as the one service industry that seems to care little for its individual clients. Although this is a big generalization, of course, most every parent will be able to identify with this statement. It's an industry where parents are continually asked to "put up and shut up." Requests for new clothes, expensive saddles and other tack, custom boots and chaps, fancy horse clothing—in addition to new horses—can be tossed at a parent at the speed of a careening bowling ball, essentially knocking down the pins of your good sense until you senselessly write the mortgage-size checks to cover it. There is absolutely nothing wrong with questioning the need for an expensive purchase. There may be a very good reason for the new tack, but you, as a consumer, deserve to understand that reason before you pay up.

Have respect for other trainers. Not everyone is an Olympian, or a perfect role model, and not everyone teaches the same or has the same game plan. But most people have something to offer someone during their lifetime, and if a trainer is honest and working hard, she should have respect from her peers. Competition spurs competitive attitudes, and everyone wants to be the winner in the ring. Simple professional courtesy and respect do a lot to lift the sport to higher levels, and this will help you and your child along the way.

Be a mentor. Some people have a rare gift that allows their knowledge and expertise to flow out of them in a seamlessly uplifting manner. This gift takes more than just good teaching skills. A mentor is someone who can inspire a student to greatness. A mentor relationship is one that will last in the child's memory for a lifetime.

Be ready to let go at the right time. See the section on moving on, page 48.

THE TOUGH STUFF: HOW TO FORGE A BETTER RELATIONSHIP

It would be a rare and wonderful thing to find a trainer with all of the above qualities, but this is the real world, and on a good day you would count yourself lucky to have a trainer with half of them. Even the most highly acclaimed and well-known trainers are sometimes as famous for other aspects of their personalities as they are for their abilities. And with any trainer, no matter how good, there will be times when you might object to her methods, or attitude, or rules, and either you have to live with it or you have to deal with it. Sometimes living with it is easier. Nobody goes through life being perfectly on time, pleasant, brilliant, and charming all at once. On our good days we can all occasionally be a little of each, but there are always days that follow where we haven't had enough sleep, we're dealing with a particularly difficult situation at home, or, in the case of your trainer, she's just given her most trying lesson of the year to the student from hell. Stuff happens. In this case, patience is the key.

But when a problem arises, or one has been there for years and you just can't bear to live with it any longer, it's good to approach it on a day when your trainer is not busy, you're not mad, and there aren't a lot of other ears to hear. Dressing down your trainer in front of her other customers is a sure way to guarantee that your relationship with her will never recover—and your child is the one likely to suffer the most. And, as anyone in management knows (or should know), dressing someone down is not good for accomplishing your goals. Here are a few alternatives:

Schedule an appointment. If your trainer doesn't have an office, ask her to join you for a cup of coffee, preferably where you can have some privacy.

Have a list of points, either on paper or firmly in your mind. Before you even go to your meeting, it's good to decide what's really bothering you. Often there may be a number of confused issues, and it's a common mistake to pick on the little things that you've been letting go. If your trainer has always been mildly tardy for lessons, but now you're mad because of some bigger issue, don't expect her to understand why you're bringing up her tardiness now after three years.

In your points, include things that you *do* like. Find some aspect of the training or the way she treats your child on which you can compliment her. *The One Minute Manager* approach from the '80s recommends that you always deliver the bad news first, then the good. The reasoning was that if you give someone a compliment followed by a "but," then that person would never learn to trust what you have to say. This approach may seem simplistic, but when your meeting is over, the last thing you've done is told her something good, and maybe that's what she'll remember.

Don't show up mad. Anger is an emotion that usually has a life of its own . . . as in out of control. And even if it's not your habit to express anger out loud, be sure that you're not steaming so much that you can't make your point rationally. If the issue is one that would fire up Mrs. Milktoast, your best means of success is a cool intellect and a frank and approachable manner.

If you are upset by something your trainer said to your child, be sure to have the facts. Even with the most scrupulously honest child, every story gets a little embellished with each telling, and you'll be quite embarrassed and frustrated to find yourself in the middle of a big "he said, she

Mad Mare Mommy.

said" game. Instead of saying, "You said such and such to my child," say, "This is what my child heard." It gives your trainer time for a graceful response. If it is indeed what she said, she can reflect and apologize without ever feeling threatened. If it's not what she said, you can reflect and apologize.

If you are upset by something your trainer said to you, nip it in the bud. You have the facts, and you can avoid further discord by saying, "Let me be sure that I heard you correctly . . ." The horse industry is famous (or infamous) for the way parents and other paying customers are frequently so intimidated by their trainers that they often live with rudeness and disrespect as a necessary evil to accomplish their child's (or their own) riding aspirations. The constant conversation among parents at horse shows is how much they've had to pay for their child's pony, how they had to buy a $2,000 saddle for their ten-year-old, how the trainer wouldn't

The feud.

answer their questions, or how the trainer insisted on this or that, no questions asked. And although much of this conversation is a kind of ritual confession of how stupid we've been as adults, or what we've allowed ourselves to do in the name of our child's career, the fact that it takes place at nearly every horse show means that there is a lot more fire than smoke. Sadly, the only ones we have to blame are ourselves.

U

The Horse Show Mom: There is a particular kind of mind numbing that goes on when we're caught up in the moment of our child's competition. Every time our child wins a class, we see her standing on the Olympic podium accepting the gold for her country (and for us), so it's no wonder we're willing to rush out and buy everything her trainer says we need. No wonder we're willing to put up with so much from the Bella Karolyis of the horse world, so that we can help shoot our child's rising star over the moon.

It happens most often at horse shows, where there are plenty of new things to buy. And often we run to the trainers ourselves, to suggest any number of new things to help our child along, particularly when we see another child more perfectly tacked up or outfitted, and that child is beating our child in end-of-year honors points.

TOUGHER STILL: WHEN IT'S TIME TO MOVE ON

Great trainers can take kids from an early age through the pinnacle of their high-school "junior" show career or beyond. Over the years, a nice, comfy synergy can develop between parent, child, and trainer, and any little speed bumps along the road are quickly forgiven and forgotten. Other times you finally acknowledge that your tolerance for your trainer's bad habits, bad humor, or bad business has dried up, and you decide it's time to move on.

Or you realize that your trainer is not the one your child needs to continue to the top. How will you know this? After a few years of horse show experience, you may notice that the children your child has been competing against are constantly in the top ribbons while your daughter is still

The tack store addiction.

struggling to place. You may also notice that the other trainers have their kids and horses better turned out. Those riders may have a "flair" or style that is not only noticed but also works well with their horses. You may talk to other parents and learn that their trainers are doing things that you've never seen your trainer do with your child, whether it be more flat work, riding without stirrups, or jumping gymnastics. Whatever the reason, a little lightbulb will start to glow in your head until you can't ignore it, and you will want to go investigate the competition.

But, first things first. Before you burn the bridge to your trainer, be sure that what you seek is really something you can achieve. A child who does not have natural talent can make up for it with a dedicated spirit and work ethic. If she lacks the former *and* the latter, ditching your trainer is not the answer. As a matter of fact, it's the wrong question, too. The question is, why is she still riding and competing? If she just wants to have fun and spend some time with horses, there are many ways to do this without the pressure of competing, not to mention the attendant expenses.

But if, in fact, you have a talented child who is frustrated by her inability to achieve the success she wants, you have a good reason to move. Some trainers, as good as they are for beginners, may not be the best teacher for your child as she grows in her ability. Some know this about themselves and are happy to let you go, even helping you find the next step in your child's training. But human nature being what it is, and egos being a big part of that nature (and just in case you hadn't already noticed, a huge part of the horse show world), you may find yourself in the difficult predicament of having to break the news to your trainer that you want to move on.

There is no easy out. You could simply walk away and never look back, but due to the close fraternity of the horse show world, such a lapse in manners could come back to do more damage to your child's ambitions than the few moments of unpleasantness that you escaped for yourself.

So what's the best method? Simple, honest truth. Lay out your child's aspirations and tell your trainer that you appreciate all that she's done, but you've decided to move on to another situation that would better suit your child's needs. If she wants to help you find another trainer, great. If you've

Saying goodbye.

already found one, but it's one she doesn't approve of, listen and thank her for her input. She may have good reason for such input, and you can investigate it later. This interview will take about five minutes and, though you both may suffer some awkward embarrassment, the trainer will appreciate that you took the time to consider her feelings.

In the end, trainers are no different from the general population. We all like to be appreciated, thanked, and recognized for things we do right. Because trainers are sometimes taking so much of our money, we often forget that money is not the same as a simple "thank you." It's a good habit to instill in children, but will never become a habit unless they see us providing the example. All relationships need tending, and tending this one pays pretty much the same rewards as tending others.

Buying and Selling Your Horse or Pony

Your daughter loves her riding lessons, but there is nothing for her to ride on non-lesson days. Or she wants to go to a horse show, but she can't take twenty-three-year-old Pudgy the Pony. Or your trainer informs you that your child is so-oo-oo talented that you would be crazy not to encourage her budding Olympic aspirations. So, what do you do? You buy her a horse, of course, or a pony.

Perhaps that wasn't the answer you were looking for. Lacking other creative alternatives, such as quitting the lessons, denying your truly exceptional child everything she desires, or seeing if a big dog would do (it won't), you set about the process of trying to find something to purchase, or possibly lease. Or, if you're lucky, find a giveaway. (Stay tuned—things are rarely "free" in life, and never in this sport.)

Buying a horse or pony for your child will introduce you to the more peculiar economic aspects of the equestrian sport. In addition to the emotional investment you might normally make on acquiring a pet (which, by the way, a horse is not) and the fretful worries about getting the best mount your pocketbook can afford, you are beginning to walk down a path from which there is usually no return. The land around you seems as if it should belong to Alice or to Dorothy, but you can bet you haven't seen a movie about this one.

Alice and Dorothy in Horse Buying Land.

Nothing in your previous life experience can prepare you for the purchase of your child's first horse or pony. Not buying a house or car or boat, and certainly not buying a dog or cat. The first word of warning should be that no matter how high the purchase price, the keeping price will always be higher. Show horses of any discipline come with the expectation that they will help your child fulfill her competitive dreams, and not only does the market bear what the deepest pockets can pay, the keeping and showing of a competitive mount is dear, very dear.

No purchasing process is simple and uncomplicated. If you have a trainer help you buy that pony, expect to pay an additional 10 to 15 percent in commission. In addition, when you sell that pony, you may be expected to pay this same commission, even though the new buyer is also paying her trainer a commission. What does this mean in practical terms? A $10,000 pony costs you $11,000, but the seller (who pays her trainer $1,000) only gets $9,000. In addition to the purchase price and commission, you will also be expected to pay any travel expenses incurred in searching for that perfect pony, as well as the price of the pre-purchase vet exam (even if the pony failed the exam and you don't buy that one). And, when your child is ready to move on to a bigger or more experienced mount, you can count on this fact of life: You may never be able to sell the pony for what you paid for it, and if you do, you will still lose money due to the commission.

In your life before horse shows, you would expect to pay a commission to the agent who sold your house, but not when you buy the new house. Your car salesman receives his commission from the dealer even though it's hidden in your purchase price, but not another commission when you sell the car back to him. The only other place where a transaction takes money out of both ends is the stock market, but at least in the stock market there is a greater chance that the stock will go up—a rare occurrence for horses, at least where parents are concerned. But get used to it if you can, because that is how it is always done.

Is this fair? Well, yes and no. A commission to a trainer who has spent her time looking for the perfect mount for your child is completely fair. Sometimes the amount of time spent involves weeks of phone calls, looking at videos, and spending time away from the barn where she could be earning money giving lessons. Also, you are getting your trainer's endorsement for a purchase that you may be sensibly unqualified to make. It is practically impossible to make a good judgment on what kind of mount your child needs, what is safe or isn't, and what would be the best competitive mount for her, if you are not an experienced horseperson yourself. A good and reputable trainer will also take care that the pony receives the best training so your child can make reasonable progress in the show ring. And very often a good trainer is willing to work out an adjusted commission just to make the deal go through.

When the prices get higher, the commissions can jump to 15 percent, so the amount your trainer is making is much greater, and probably for the same amount of time. The difference is that your expectations of a good result are higher. If you are having your trainer buy you a serious five-figure horse, or even a six-figure horse, you need to be sure that she is experienced enough to do so. The horse show world is truly telepathic; as soon as the word is out that someone is reaching deep into his or her pockets, every trainer and agent suddenly has a stable of six-figure horses. Many of these horses will be legitimately worth that price, but many will not. Your trainer's skill and expertise is critical here, and it's best if you know that she has had successful experience in the buying of expensive horses. You wouldn't want a young intern performing open-heart surgery on you, but you'd be happy to pay the asking price for an experienced cardiac surgeon to do the job correctly. Take a look around the barn and see what kind of horses the trainer has purchased for other clients. Are the clients happy with the trainer's choices? Do they feel that they got the best mount for their money? If the answer is yes, then you can be fairly well assured that you will have the same experience. If the answer is no, and every stall has a revolving door as the trainer keeps searching for better horses, then you might have a talk with her about networking with a more experienced trainer (even if she has to share the commission) to help her find what you need.

Another quirk in this endeavor is that you as the buyer are often expected to remain uninvolved in the process. This may be the hardest thing of all. What seems as if it should be a simple negotiating process turns into a clogged communications network of parents, trainers, buyers, sellers, and other trainers, when all the poor little kid wants is just a pony.

THE HORSE SHOW MOM: LESSONS LEARNED
Haggling

The second pony we purchased for our daughter involved some price haggling. My astute businessman husband was astonished to find out that he was not allowed to call the seller and haggle it out over the phone. I remember driving home with our trainer, trying to make the deal work: I would call my husband, then our trainer would call the seller's trainer, the seller's trainer would call the seller, and back and forth, back and forth, for at least an hour. All my husband wanted to do was call the little girl's dad and talk it out, man-to-man. Instead, we had to jam all the cell towers between Kansas City and Iowa. The dads could have worked it out in five minutes and we would still have paid the trainer's commission, although, in our case, our trainer was happy to make an adjustment just to get off the phone. So in a lot of ways, the whole thing gets quite silly. Any horse show parent who has been through this would agree, but for some reason we still put up and shut up, or else risk being labeled "difficult show parents." In a world where all the money flows from the parents (who are usually highly competent business people) it's a sociological phenomenon to find such insecurity.

Another problem that arises in horse buying and selling is that as trainers ask around for horses, many people start sticking their hands out for a little grease. Though many trainers will happily pass along the knowledge of a special horse to their friends in the industry, just as many others ask for a part of the action, either for passing along a video or often just for the referral. The practice drives your price up, and this is when the answer to "Is it fair?" ends up being a resounding no.

So what can you do? Tell your trainer in advance how much you think you can reasonably spend and that you would like the best value for what you can spend, which means you won't have extra money for a lot of middlemen. This will alert your trainer that you are serious about the purchase, but you are also cautious. When you ask a trainer to act as your agent in the purchase or sale of a horse, the trainer and you have entered into an agreement where the agent (trainer) is legally bound to act in your best interests. You can specify what these "best interests" are. You should also ask for and expect a reasonable estimate of additional costs incurred that relate to the horse purchase, such as travel, lodging, and pre-purchase vet exam.

———————————— U ————————————

The Horse Show Mom: Stories abound in the horse world about the many palms that receive a kickback. It is usually the buyer that gets stuck—sometimes knowingly, sometimes unwittingly. I heard of a parent whose trainer had found the perfect pony for his child, only to find that there was an extra commission involved for someone only mildly connected to the sale. This someone had given the trainer a phone number and then expected a $1,000 thank-you. The trainer's commission was exactly $1,000, so either she'd have to hand it over or the parent would. At this point, with the blessings of the trainer, the parent pulled the plug with a "No, thank you." It may have disappointed his child, but it sent the message that a phone number is not worth $1,000. As it was also a lost commission for the seller's trainer, it surely put the friendly "phone number" guy in the horse world doghouse—at least for a while.

Pre-purchase Vet Exam

When your child has tried a pony or horse and you and the trainer are happy with how she is riding it, the best thing that can happen is that you can take the pony home to your barn or the trainer's barn for a two-week trial. It's not always an option, but it's worth asking for. If any quirks are about to happen, it's better they happen during a trial period than after you've written the check. This trial can happen only if you are serious about the purchase and after an offer has been made to the seller, conditional on the pony working out at home.

Once the trial is over and it's a success, or if you choose to forgo the trial, the pony then gets a pre-purchase exam by a vet. Depending upon the pony's price, this could be a simple exam or one involving X-rays. It should always involve testing for drugs, which should happen immediately after your child has ridden the pony. There is absolutely no way one can tell just by looking if a horse or pony has been tranquilized or given anti-inflammatory drugs to cover up a lameness problem. A good rule of thumb: It's much cheaper to get a full vet exam than to pay lifetime board on a lame horse (or a psycho pony) that you can't sell or even give away. You need to speak with the vet, in addition to the trainer, about his findings during the exam. Even though the trainer may have more experience understanding the vet's findings, you should make a knowledgeable consideration of your purchase so that you may be informed for your child's sake as well as for any future sale. You may love and trust your trainer completely, but life changes, and next week or next year you could be out looking for another barn without any knowledge of your pony's special needs.

Not every negative finding is a deal breaker, either. An older—but safe—pony should be expected to have some arthritis issues, and it will take supplements and other vet work to keep the pony comfortable for riding and showing.

∪

The Horse Show Mom: A young rider in our barn found a wonderful horse with a glandular problem that interfered with the horse's sweating. This was a manageable health problem that actually put the price within reach of this hardworking youngster. Horse and rider went on to enjoy each other immensely, both in and out of the show ring.

Often, once the deal is set, you as the buyer will make a payment to the seller, then to the trainer for commission and expenses. The vet will bill you directly. If your trainer wants a check made out to her for the total purchase price, it is absolutely your right to ask her for full disclosure of any payments made to any other party. As an agent, she is legally bound to disclose these to you. This will limit the amount of "grease" coming out of your pocket as the buyer for all those helping hands along the way.

Though most trainers are reputable and honest, the horse show world is filled with stories of parents who think they just sold their daughter's pony for $50,000, but the buyer paid $100,000 plus commission. It needs to happen only a couple of times to become the horse show world's favorite urban legend, but it does happen, and you don't want it happening to you.

ONCE YOU GET THE PONY HOME

The purchase of a new horse or pony—we'll consider them interchangeably—is usually fraught with expectations and big dreams of success. If this is a first pony, the world you've just entered will keep you learning and on your toes for quite some time. Bonding with a new pony takes time; getting familiar with all of the pony's quirks, manners, likes, and dislikes is a learning process from which you will never totally graduate. As a species, horses do not fit into our normal experience of children, dogs, cats, or other pets. They are flight animals that have been highly domesticated, but still

First pony.

retain their basic impulses: to run off when scared or startled, to keep grazing even though you want them to come in, and to constantly fit into the hierarchy of their herd. As your child (and you) bond with her pony, your daughter will become a member of the herd, and hopefully, the leader. It is an important accomplishment when your daughter's pony begins to accept her as the leader, whether on the ground when she's grooming or in the saddle when she's riding. And no matter how good the combination of horse and rider gets, there will be off days for both of them—and often not at the same time—so patience is the key when the new pony comes home, either to your house or your boarding place.

This is also the time when you need your trainer the most. Good beginnings in a rider/horse relationship are the key to all of the possible successes down the road, and even if you have the pony at home, lessons are critical at this juncture. Every horse or pony has its own special little way of doing things, and responds to rider's aids just a tad differently. Some hate spurs, while others were never ridden without spurs. Some need to be lunged a little before ridden; some are petrified of the crop; some are "cold-backed" and twitchy when being saddled; others try to bite when being cinched. Your trainer's long years of experience will be invaluable now when your child is becoming used to her pony and the little ways in which she needs to adjust her position or her attitude for the best possible outcome.

MOVING UP

If this is your second, or third, or even fourth time around with a new horse or pony, your expectations may be lower for immediate bonding, but greater for the amount of success this newly formed duo will accomplish in the show arena. The reason for getting yet another horse, or "trading up" (though sometimes for size only), as any experienced horse show parent can tell you, is usually because the previous mount could not take the child to the next level of competitive success. There are wonderful, talented horses, "Old Faithfuls" who can win over three-foot jumps, but not higher; horses that can be Training Level or First Level champions year after year, but have problems with flying lead changes, and who cannot move up the dressage ladder. While these accomplishments are very good at one stage, if your child is talented and you have the means, you do what any self-respecting horse show parent would do: you try to get the best horse your money can buy for that next level.

This means that unless you are in the uncommon position of being able to afford to keep every mount your daughter ever owned, you will also need to sell her previous mount. As mentioned in the beginning of this chapter, this comes with the possibility of financial loss. It takes some very savvy dealing and knowledge of horses, not to mention a very fat wallet, to speculate with your child's horses or ponies and actually come out a winner. Usually, one would consider themselves lucky to get the initial investment back (and don't forget, your "investment" is never the stated purchase price).

Whatever the outcome, this period can be a tense time between you and your child's trainer. Not only are you shopping for the next perfect mount, but you are also worried that her current mount won't sell. Some parents are very good about waiting until the old one sells before even looking for another. Others get involved in the frenzy that happens once it's known that the wonderful next-level horse, "Wins A Lot," has just come on the market, and they're convinced there will never be another opportunity like this one. There is sometimes pressure from the trainer to not let this opportunity pass, while other times the trainer is trying to convince the parent that "Wins A Lot" won't win for her daughter (this can be true for many reasons, not the least of which may be your child's ability, as hard as that is to take).

The most sensible thing, of course, if money matters (and when doesn't it?) is to wait until you've found a home for "Old Faithful." If "Old Faithful" is sound and serviceable, there should be no reason why you can't sell, and hopefully, at a suitable price. If it's not "Old Faithful" you're trying to sell, but a "Young Thing" that just didn't work out for your child, you may consider having someone else show him to get a good competition record going (if you can afford to). This might be necessary in order to get your price. Of course, this is the horse world, and there are no guarantees that this strategy will work; but if you can do it on a reasonable budget and your trainer thinks it is worth a shot, then proceed, but with caution.

If, after a couple of shows, "Young Thing" is still underperforming, you may want to quit the showing and proceed with finding a good buyer and home. Very often, with young horses that are talented and who came with high expectations, there is someone out there who will think he's fantastic, even without a solid show record. Your trainer's reputation and networking abilities come into play here, and will hopefully reap the results that you desire.

ALTERNATIVES TO SELLING

Every so often, and actually more often than that, a horse is just impossible to sell. You may be in a limited market for that type of horse, your trainer may not be well known or may lack the confidence to extend herself to unknown trainers, or (as is mostly the case in this scenario) your horse may be dangerous, lame, or too old for the job. And you may be desperately trying not to be responsible for his board for the rest of his life, which might be longer than your child's show career.

There are other options besides selling, some with (and some without) financial reward:

1. If you have a mare, you may consider offering her to someone to breed. This would require a mare that is young enough and worthy of breeding and as such, desirable to a breeder. The breeder may pay all of her expenses in exchange for the foals she produces. If you are lucky, you may even get a lease fee over and above the expenses. Without a fee you could require the breeder to keep her through her retirement until she passes away. You could draw up an agreement that would state such terms and the level of care you expect to receive.

2. You could give the horse away. If your horse is simply older and unable to do the job you need him for, you might be able to find a farm or stable that is looking for a useful and safe school horse, but can't afford to invest anything in its purchase.

3. If you've spent a considerable amount on this horse, you may be able to donate him to a nonprofit riding program such as a therapeutic riding program in exchange for some tax benefit. Your accountant can advise you as to the legitimacy of any such programs, and your trainer can investigate the care received and whether your horse and this program are a good match.

4. If your horse is too difficult for such a program, you could possibly donate him to a college equestrian program where he will be ridden by more experienced riders. There may or may not be tax benefits.

5. You could find a farm with plenty of property that accepts "retirement" horses for a monthly fee. This is a good match if your horse has a serious lameness problem and will never be able to work again. The

monthly fees, while not zero, are usually cheaper than any barn board you could find. The care can be good, although horses normally live outside.

Explore the options with your trainer, and remember that years of board, shoes, and vet bills will add up more quickly than the lost purchase price. In this case, "cutting your losses" becomes a literal term.

SAYING GOOD-BYE

Normally, a pet is kept like a family member until it passes away. This is a sad time, but one of life's certainties, and the grief is expected. One sells a horse or pony usually to accommodate a new mount or to send a child off to college, so this particular rite of passage can happen every couple of years (or more often) in the life of your child's show career. The grief, however, can be as great or greater than the final passing of a beloved pet. The relationship your child has with her horse may not be as physically intimate as the one she shares with Sheba the cat who sleeps in her bed, but the emotional intimacy based on that unique horse/rider team, the expectations they have had of each other, and the rewards and accomplishments they've reached together go way beyond that of a pet that is kept for comfort and companionship. So even though the relationship may only be two years old when "First Pony" or even "Second Horse" leaves the barn for a new home, the grief can be as palpable and deep as any of life's mournings.

───────────────── U ─────────────────

The Horse Show Mom: Our daughter Chétie's third pony, Ally, was not the easiest ride on the block. She was beautiful and talented, but Chétie had to learn to ride her with complete focus and skill. This was excellent for Chétie's training, but created some ambivalence in my feelings for Ally. She did great with her the first year, winning Zone Finals and qualifying for Devon. We also had a delightful time taking her to Pony Finals. She was a medium pony, and the second year, little Chétie grew more quickly than we expected, so at age twelve she had essentially outgrown the pony we thought would be useful until Chétie turned fourteen.

We sent Ally off to an agent to be sold so that we could get her something bigger. We had been through the grieving period before, and felt we knew what to expect. In Ally's last week at the barn before the shipper arrived, we bathed her, played with her in the field, and took lots of "good-bye" photos. I also blistered under the barrage of darts that shot from Chétie's tearful eyes, endured the punishing silences and subsequent meltdowns of sobs and life-gripping hugs. I experienced my own sad heart because, ambivalent or not, I loved this pony too. But what I was completely unprepared for was how my sadness would grow into its own kind of grief and last longer than Chétie's, who, a month later, was enjoying getting to know her new pony jumper. Every time the agent called with a possible buyer, there was that moment of fiscally hopeful joy, followed by a new tug of grief as I realized I might be losing Ally this time. Not surprisingly, every deal fell through, and we took Ally back after nearly two years. I now ride her as my dressage pony.

Ally's good-bye.

Parents have different approaches to saying good-bye. It can be a big affair or a quiet little moment. It can be the most difficult the first time you have to say good-bye, with the process getting easier over time, or it can worsen over time as your child realizes that this is one of the prices she has to pay as a developing competitor. You will meet parents who make little of the matter, and other parents who are appalled that a horse is sold as a commodity, the latter cherishing and caring for all of their child's horses and ponies for the rest of their lives. There is every scenario that you can imagine, and yours will be as unique as you and your child are unique in the world.

Here Comes the Judge

There is nothing more frustrating in sports than feeling that the judge, umpire, or referee has done less than a stellar job for your child. Every parent who has been involved with Little League remembers with vivid accuracy the gross inaccuracies of certain games where their child was called out (when he clearly wasn't), or when the ump's strike zone was somewhere in hell instead of across the plate. A high school basketball game, that highly emotional and energy-charged parent-as-spectator experience, is filled with as many invectives against the referees as it is with cheers for the teams. Ditto for soccer—and let's not forget the tennis kids who make their name more on their line calls than their actual skill. We've all shared in some of these experiences, and we've probably all had days when we shudder at the loud parent next to us, or we shudder on the way home realizing we *were* that parent.

The most difficult task that we face as parents of competitors is to keep everything in perspective, and not feel that:

   a. winning or losing is a reflection on us
   b. the judge is unfairly persecuting our child
   c. the judge is a personal friend of the winner's trainer
   d. the judge doesn't know what he's doing
   e. the judge was eating his lunch during our child's event
   f. the judge is an idiot

Waiting for the judge to test.

And while many parents may say, "Not me," there will be a part in each of us that finds a little bell ringing in the truth.

Some aspects of every equestrian discipline involve a certain amount of subjective judging. Dressage is all subjectively judged, even though the movements are prescribed. In eventing, there is the similarly judged dressage phase, in addition to the possibility that the jump judges, with their close-up perspective, may see things a little differently than you do. In the hunter/jumper world, all the equitation and hunter divisions are judged subjectively, as they are in the Western Breeds, which also have similar conformation classes, including Halter, Western Pleasure, and Trail, just to name a few. So the upshot of this is the clear possibility that in the same company with similar performances, two judges may prefer different horses and/or riders. It doesn't take long for Horse Show Moms or Dads to see this, but it takes a very long time indeed to understand and accept it.

U

The Horse Show Mom: I once attended a clinic with my daughter while she was still riding her pony, Ally. Most of the other participants were older and doing higher jumps, but there was a 2'6" section, and the clinician was a well-known Hunter/Equitation judge. In addition

Keeping score.

to the riding, he had classroom sessions on judging. I was able to attend them and so enjoyed hearing what he had to say about what he liked and didn't like in the hunters, and also how he would judge a class. He had all the participants judge a class at the end of the weekend, and we then compared our notes with his. It was one of the most informative weekends in all of my experience as a Horse Show Mom.

My daughter, Chétie, got to do an experiment for him. She put in a really good round in an equitation class, in which almost everyone placed her first. (As her mom, I had to recuse myself from this section.) When the clinician ended up placing her last, we were all amused to hear that he had privately asked her ahead of time to drop her stirrup when she was on the other side of the arena, where none of us in the stands could see (losing a stirrup is an automatic elimination in Equitation). He could see it, of course, because of where he was seated.

Along with a few good pony mom friends, I spent the rest of that winter horse show season glued to the bleachers in the pony ring, judging sheets in hand, privately judging every pony class and comparing it to the official outcome. We were all stunned to see that with a lot of attention, we could clearly see how most of the classes would come out. We might be off by one or two points, which could be chalked up to personal preference, but we basically agreed with the judge.

THE GENERAL PICTURE

In all Hunter and Western conformation type classes, the most important element is the horse; how he is built, the way he goes, and how he is groomed and turned out are all essential elements to the picture. No matter how good your child is, the horse needs to be better than the other horses in the class. In any equitation type class, where the rider is being judged, the judge can be a little more forgiving of the horse's type, though turnout and grooming, tack and show shine are also elements of the rider's equitation abilities. The rider's skill is paramount, however, and as such, the best performance should win. In dressage, the horse's talent counts for a lot as horse and rider move up the levels, but again, the rider needs the skills to perform the tasks at hand.

Then why does your daughter sometimes place first and sometimes place last? In any competition, the placing depends more on the other competition than just the particular skill of your child or the conformation of her horse. She can compete in a class of twenty and come out on top, but in a class of ten with more talented competitors, she might place only sixth. This is where it gets hard to keep the more detached Horse Show Mom composure.

Once our child wins a few classes, we begin to think of her in that way. "Oh, yeah, she's the winner, uh huh." "Glad we got her that expensive con-

Judging conformation.

formation pony." "So glad we got last year's top event horse for her." It can be a bit mortifying to watch her blow a class and come out last, but the frustration we feel if this becomes the norm can inspire a little unloading on the judge, particularly if the child is putting in relatively decent rounds and still not getting ribbons. Here is when paying very close attention to the others in the class can soothe your feelings of frustration and put that aggravation to better use. Pretend you are the judge, take very good notes on each class, and see how you come out. Read up on your discipline's judging requirements. Find some friends to sit in the stands with you and judge (ask your husband to do so). Chances are more likely that you find the judging is fairly even overall, if not totally fair, than that the judge always has some other agenda.

However, there are those times when it all seems totally cockamamie, and you and a lot of the other parents think you ended up on the planet Mars of horse shows. It does happen, and probably not so rarely, that some judges have a little conflict of interest going on. How hard would it be for a judge to place last the fancy horse he sold six months ago to the client in the ring? Really hard, unless he's Solomon. And without some gross and obvious error on the rider's part, there may be a little favoritism in the placings. It shouldn't happen, but it does. We all hear about it; and while parents and trainers alike discuss it, nothing ever seems to be done about it. The question is, how much does it matter, and *can* we do anything about it?

In the great scheme of things, it probably doesn't matter much. Judges rarely judge the same venue over and over, week after week. They usually travel around a lot, and unless they are on the exact same show schedule as your barn, you'll run into that judge only occasionally; and the chances that the same judge/competitor combination will be at each show is even less likely.

If there is a major error on the judge's part, such as placing first a competitor who made such a huge mistake that everyone is up in arms, something *should* be done about it. And although in this case, the placing may never be changed, at least the judge is put on notice that quite a few people think he erred. However, that is not the job for Horse Show Mom. No trainer would feel comfortable letting an irate parent approach the judge. In each discipline, there are venues for lodging complaints, whether with the judge himself, the Technical Delegate (TD), or the steward. Your trainer can and should do this for you if she also feels it's justified. Some trainers may feel timid to do so because of worry over their own reputation, but to allow gross errors to go unchallenged is not good for the sport. A trainer with a good reputation can approach a steward or TD without fear of reprisal of any kind.

Judging any discipline is not easy. Judges often have horrible weather to contend with, sitting either in freezing rain or in a hot judge's box on a hundred-degree summer's day. Minimal breaks, crummy food, and thankless competitors make the job completely unenviable. Years of experience, dedication to the sport, travel away from home—not to mention a pretty thick skin—are a few of the things necessary to become a good judge. And many beginner judges are on their way to becoming great ones, even though their road may be filled with some potholes of bad judgment and missed calls. Respect for this hard work and devotion is as important for us to give as it is for our child to see being given. There are plenty of spoiled kids and poor losers out there, who have little respect for the judge's opinion. We certainly don't need to multiply the species.

CHAPTER

7

Horse Show Dads

Writing a book titled *The Horse Show Mom's Survival Guide* has brought some amusing questions and looks from my husband, Bob. He seems to think that I've forgotten (or ignored) the fact that he, as a dad, is also involved. I haven't forgotten; it's just that, well, guys are different, and as such, deserve their own chapter.

Horse Show Moms are a singular breed. No matter the discipline, we can identify each other outside the show grounds by our clothes and demeanor. Wearing dusty clogs or scuffed-up cowboy boots, cruising the farm store, tack store, or Wal-Mart, we can spot each other from aisles away. There is a certain determined look in our eyes as we search for another hoof pick, a little gleam if there is a promising new equine shampoo, positive grins for the clipper blade markdowns, and sighs of resignation (but not indignation) at the final checkout tally. At horse shows we swap stories about our trainers, complain about the judging, make excuses for our kids' mistakes in the arena ("she's really a much better rider, she's just having an off day"), rehash every round until it has been analyzed with more precision than a Wall Street adviser would give to the stock of the year, and still have more to talk about the next day. And all with a continually fresh outlook and sense of eagerness.

Dads, on the other hand, are another breed entirely, but within this breed there are a few different types. The first one is the nonparticipating dad. This subset of dads love their kids, but hate the sport. Horses are so foreign to them and the competitions so boring, you couldn't pay them to attend, except for the most important finals of the year. Even then, you can expect them to have their noses buried in the newspaper or a book every moment when their kid is not on the field or in the ring. Nor are they interested in meeting other dads in the sport; they are afraid they might catch some weird horse-loving disease and succumb to the same madness as the rest of the family.

Another type is the dad who is tolerant of the sport. These dads make a good effort to enjoy the sport, show up occasionally when they can, try not to rant on forever about the expense, and really enjoy it when their kid wins. My husband belongs to this type. Being a very natural Little League dad type, he's happy to get to watch some kind of kid competition now that

Horse Show Dad and daughter: Brian and Hanna McLean.

our baseball-, soccer-, tennis-playing son has grown up. He even takes our daughter, Chétie, to a show every year or two, by himself, which seems to astonish him more than it does me, finding it surprising to show up at a venue that is totally foreign to him. There are no noisy, rowdy parents screaming at their kids from the stands. No one yelling, "Hey, batter, batter." No wild brawls with the soccer coach who just lost the game; and more importantly, few other dads with whom to commiserate.

Our son played baseball from the time he was seven all the way through high school. Some years my husband was assistant coach, and other years his business schedule kept him out of town too much to make the commitment. This was a bit frustrating for him, so in order to have some involvement, he took up scorekeeping, which was relatively satisfying as it gave him an official role; he got to sit in the dugout, and he could stay really focused on the game. That is generally not an option with horse show competition, except for eventing, where dads can be jump judges (which is not much different from the lowly job of base coach at a ball game: People can argue with your call, nobody respects you, and thanks can be rare).

For most dads, and ours particularly, horse shows are the sporting scene from hell: no yelling, weird judging, interminable waiting for the all-too-short two minutes in the arena, and quite often a 90 percent female audience. What's a guy to do? Turn to the lady next to him and say, "I really love your daughter's hunt coat"? "Beautiful half-pass"? "Who did your horse's braids"? Not the conversation of preference for most guys. I know my husband would prefer to be at the rail, shouting, "Go, Chétie! That's the way to clear the jumps!" He'd like to yell at the judge occasionally, too, something like: "What are you, nuts? That was a beautiful equitation round. What were you thinking?!!" Of course, he'd have to *know* what a beautiful equitation round looked like, but nonetheless, it would give him so much more satisfaction if he could vent some of his pent-up Little League emotions.

Instead, Bob makes do with what he has to work with. He flirts a little with the other moms, and occasionally finds a dad he can commiserate with; comparing horse prices, the best truck for hauling, trailering horror stories, and mostly, the latest sports scores (not the equestrian type). Horse Show Moms love this kind of dad. He gets an "A" for effort, and we as moms can go back to chatting with each other about what's really important: the best boot repair shops, the latest craze in kid and horse show mom jewelry, what the snooty kid at the barn said to our kid, and how close we are in points to qualifying for finals. We can also wax on forever about our horses, brag about our kids' grades, and—when we're really good—we can laugh at ourselves and the whole process.

The third kind of dad is one member of a pair of two wildly enthusiastic horse show parents, Horse Show Mom and Horse Show Dad. They are a rare breed indeed; so rare that no generalization can be made about them. I've

Horse Show Dad at the in-gate.

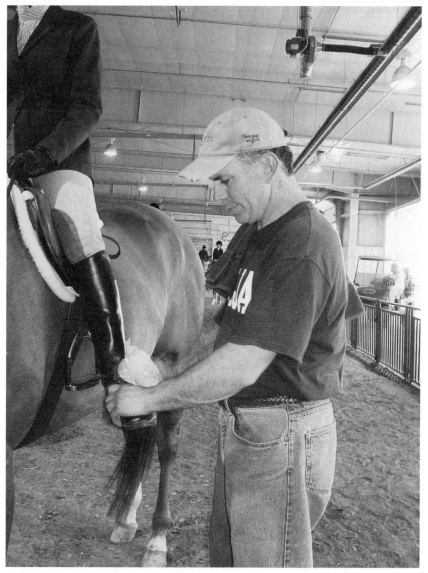

Horse Show Dads can polish boots, too.

seen them, so I know they exist. I've watched them loading horses, working in tandem, grooming and polishing boots. But I don't really know them. As a matter of fact, I can't be sure they aren't a figment of my imagination.

The fourth kind of dad is in a realm all his own: the male counterpart to a Horse Show Mom—the professional Horse Show Dad. He's the one who drives the horses, spends the weekend with the kids, polishes boots, grooms the horse, knows all about tack and where each piece goes, gives pep talks, and astonishes most of the moms at the show. Perhaps his wife can't make it, perhaps she can't relate, but for whatever reason, there he is, like the rest of us moms, doing the job we love best, and usually doing a better job of it. He's a kind of lone ranger. Often, these dads have no sons. Without ball games to root for, they get on the bandwagon of their daughter's sport so they can participate, and they do—to the max. I am in awe of these dads. They often know more than I do, complain less than I do, have more patience with their kids than I do, and their perspective on the sport can be, well, cosmic. I even met one dad who changed his profession just so he could go to horse shows with his daughter, an only child. He has my lifelong admiration.

But, the question is, which type would I prefer to be married to? Well, the second type, of course. Nowhere in my life is there room for a person more horse show obsessed than I am. And this is how it usually works, one parent per sport: one to recount to the other all of the day's details in minutiae, and one less-interested parent to keep perspective on the bigger picture of life (the one who stays at home, worrying about the bills and missed school days). In other words, one parent for balance, one non-horse show obsessed partner to grow old with, one partner just like mine.

Western Breeds

Of all the riding disciplines, none has been so romanticized as Western. For those of us baby boomers who grew up in the city, the Western horse is close to the hearts of our own childhood memories of movie and song, and to our grandparents' memories of the horse in practical use. For those fortunate enough to grow up on cattle ranches, the horse has been a working family member whose education is as valued as that of the human constituents. And much like the old days of mounted battle, when armies trained their cavalry in times of peace by developing training techniques and competitions to keep their troops fresh (such as eventing), so has the Western horse become a competitive animal, seeking glory outside the cattle range at home. The rodeo is the most recognizable of the Western sports, but from there to the show arena, there are many layers of competitive sport of different styles and goals. The costumes and saddles are fit for the wealthiest cattle barons, and the horses are bred for the best competitive results.

A parent new to this sport may be overwhelmed by the choices. The number, variety of classes, and training choices for your child are vast, as are the showing opportunities. Unlike dressage, eventing, and hunter/jumpers, the Western breeds are not all managed under the one organizational umbrella of the United States Equestrian Federation (USEF). Although some Western shows fall under the USEF's jurisdiction, the breeds rule in the Western arena, with each breed having its own showing organization, venues, prizes, and year-end awards. Breed shows offer classes in Western horsemanship, halter, trail, jumping, roping, cattle classes, speed events, and even English hunters and jumpers.

Starting at the top is the American Quarter Horse, with its 350,000-plus members of the American Quarter Horse Association (AQHA). These wonderful horses are bred to be compact, heavily muscled, light on their feet, agreeable in temperament, and fast—very fast—with the ability to stop on a dime. Quarter Horses are raced, jumped, reined, used for hunting as well as dressage work, and shown in hand for conformation. The revered subject of nearly every song written for or by cowboys, they are the great living American icon.

Their close sibling, the American Paint Horse, with Quarter Horse and/or Thoroughbred background, is a separate and distinctive breed, with all of the wonderful qualities of its origins plus the added value of its color. Certain required bloodlines, plus the right amount of color, qualifies these horses for membership in the 100,000-plus member American Paint Horse Association (APHA). Splashes of white over sorrel, bay, chestnut, or black make this horse a catch for any eye, and most little girls (and boys) sigh with desire on their first encounter.

Many other breeds compete in Western breed shows. Appaloosas, Pony of the Americas, and Pintos are the most prevalent breeds. Arabians also compete, as do Morgans, Palominos, and some Saddlebreds, although these breeds compete in a variety of other classes. Each breed has its own organizations and shows. Just to further confuse the newcomer, there are "all breed" shows where any breed can compete. For all of these, most have classes for Halter (conformation), Leadline, Showmanship, Western Pleasure, Western Riding, Horsemanship, hunter under saddle and over fences, Jumpers, Equitation, and of course, all the speed events, including pole bending and barrel racing. For the working horses there are classes in reining, roping, cutting, and the list goes on.

If your child is already riding and taking lessons, your trainer will fill you in on the types of shows she normally attends. You may be at a barn that is all Quarter Horses, or mostly Paints, or a mix of those with some Appaloosas. Trainers may go to some AQHA shows, and also some open shows or local shows. Not to worry; in Western, there is a venue for everyone.

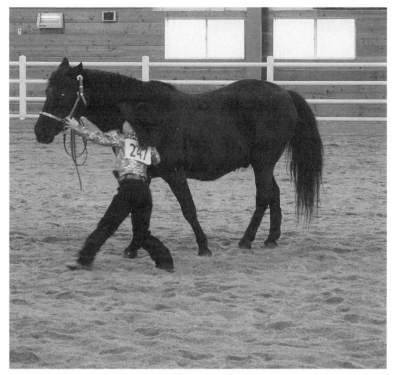

Jacque Murray and pony.

Like all other disciplines, your child will start by learning the basics: walk, jog (Western lingo for a slower version of the trot), and lope (that's the canter). For showing, she may be competing when she's quite young in classes for little tykes that include leadline and walk-trot classes. As she develops, her trainer may encourage her to try Showmanship, where she will lead her pony or horse into the ring and show the judge her skill in getting him to do a required test, such as walking and jogging in hand, backing up, halting squarely, and turning around. The moves become more difficult and exacting as she progresses in age, but it's a great beginning, and there is nothing quite as endearing as a five-year-old all decked out in beautiful show gear tugging on the halter of her recalcitrant pony, or performing in her first equitation class, with mom in a matching outfit holding the lead line.

A good first step is to attend a horse show or two with your child before she is actually ready to show. With over 350,000 members in the AQHA alone, you can be sure that there are either local shows or sanctioned (official) shows nearby, and that they occur frequently. Because there are so many different types of classes, your child can get an idea of what appeals to her, and you can see (with your trainer) what might be a good match for your child and her horse. Showmanship, equitation, and horsemanship classes are a must for learning basic skills as she moves up. She may find she loves the slow precision of Western Pleasure, the thrill of jumping a course, or the speed classes like pole bending and barrel racing, and not be the least bit interested in English equitation or hunters, or she may be eager for the whole shebang as she tries for the All-Around High Point Award. Whatever the case, you are in for a lot of fun—albeit exhausting fun—as you help change clothes and tack for each different event all day long.

A BEGINNER'S WESTERN GLOSSARY

This beginner's glossary will help you with the rest of the chapter. For a more complete list of terms, see the glossary in the back of the book.

Billet: A piece of leather that hooks the saddle to the cinch. (Or what you say to your trainer when you are out of money.)

Bosal: (pronounced bo-SAL) This unusual-looking piece of tack, with a lot of rope and horsehair knots, is part of a Western bitless bridle.

Change of lead: When changing direction at the lope, the horse balances himself by changing the leading leg. This can be done by walking or trotting through the change; when it's done instantly, it's called a flying change.

Chaps: Leather leggings that fit over regular pants or jeans. They are beneficial in their ability to keep one's legs in the saddle and against the horse.

Cinch: The belt-like strap that goes around the belly of the horse and attaches to the saddle (via the billet and the off billet) to keep the saddle in place.

Cinchy: A term for a horse that dislikes being cinched up.

Conformation: The way a horse is put together. All breeds have their ideal, so in a conformation class, the judge compares your horse to the ideal type.

Cues: The signals the rider gives to her horse through the seat, hands, or legs. English riders call them aids. Spurs and whips are known as artificial aids.

Exhibitor: Anyone participating in a horse show or event.

Forehand: The part of the horse in front of the saddle. Usually used in relation to a required movement, as in "a turn on the forehand," in which the horse uses his hind legs to circle around while his front legs stay in place.

Gaits: The horse's different pace of forward movements: walk, jog, lope, or gallop.

Hack: This is a crossover term with a different meaning in each discipline. In Western lingo, a hunter "hack" is a type of horse well suited to the hunter classes. It is also the name of a class that includes jumping two fences and demonstrating a flying change of lead.

Halter: The term used for both a type of class at a horse show and a piece of tack-like equipment. A horse shown in a "halter" class is judged on his conformation. A "halter" restrains a riderless horse and is used in place of a bridle in this instance. It can be made of leather or nylon.

Headstall: The part of the bridle that goes over the horse's head and keeps the bit in his mouth—not a hole in the wall for a horse's head!

Horsemanship: A class in which the rider's form and control are judged.

Hunter: A "type," not breed, of a horse. A hunter type is well balanced, going forward at a willing pace, with head traveling relaxed but slightly elevated. The optimum leg motion reaches forward in long smooth strides that are relatively straight from the hip.

Jog: The trot in Western lingo; a somewhat slower and less elevated version than its English riding counterpart.

Jump out: Showing out of your horse trailer for a day. Your horse stays tied up by the trailer and doesn't require a stall.

Latigo: Long strips of leather used in Western tack, most often to secure rain slickers to the back of a saddle.

Lead: A term with several meanings: A "lead" rope or shank attaches to a halter. A handler "leads" a horse into the show arena for halter classes. Or, the common term for the correct "leading leg" at the lope.

Lope: The canter in Western lingo; a slower and less elevated version of its English counterpart.

Pattern: Required movements in a class where the rider or handler is being judged; often done with orange cones to indicate transition points.

Poll: Different, indeed, from a "pole" on the ground used in speed classes. It's the highest point of the horse's head right behind the ears. "Relaxed at the poll" is when the horse has flexed his neck.

Rein-back: Asking the horse to move backwards.

Sanctioned: An officially recognized show venue where points accrue for year-end awards.

Set up: Getting a horse to stand squarely on all four feet.

Shank and lead shank: The rope attached to a halter for leading a horse. It sometimes has a chain section that can be put over the nose of an unruly horse or under the chin in showmanship classes.

Showmanship: A specific class in which the handler's ability to present a horse is judged.

Trot: The English version of the jog. The trot has longer strides than the jog, and is often faster.

Wrong lead: Loping or cantering on the incorrect lead, such as the right foreleg and hind leg preceding the left ones when the horse is loping to the left.

THE SHOWS

Once you, your child, and her trainer all agree that she is ready for a show, you may find yourself at a local "open" non-sanctioned show, or you may be getting right on with her career by going to a sanctioned event. You will be introduced to the Premium List, which will have an application, a list of classes, and usually some good information about the local area. Your trainer may fill this out for you, but it's a good idea to become proficient at this job, which falls into one of the many categories of Horse Show Mom's jobs, under the heading of "secretary."

To compete at a sanctioned show, your child or your family must belong to your breed's organization. If your child is the only one competing in the family, a youth membership is the least expensive, available to anyone eighteen and under, according to the following age rule: For most breed organizations, your child is considered a youth member through the year in which she is eighteen years old on January 1. Or, in other words, whenever she is nineteen as of January 1, she must then register as an adult.

MEMBERSHIPS:

Your child and her horse must first be members to compete and accumulate points toward year-end awards. This applies to any event sanctioned by your breed. Most memberships are available online (listed at the end of this chapter, page 109), and usually at the horse shows themselves. As of 2005, the annual youth memberships for the various breeds were:

AQHA: $20.00   POAC: $52.00 (includes entire family)

APHA: $12.50   PtHA: $15.00

ApHC: $10.00

AHA: $20.00 ($35.00 USEF membership is also required if you want to show at regional and nationals finals)

Horse recordings (membership fees) for horses vary according to each breed. You can usually purchase yearly or lifetime recordings. Check your breed handbook for details.

For each of the classes covered in this chapter, there is a corresponding rule reference for the following breeds: Quarter Horse (AQHA), Paint Horse (APHA), Appaloosas (ApHC), Pony of the Americas (POAC), and American Pinto Horse Association (PtHA). Arabian Horse Association (AHA) classes are covered in the United States Equestrian Federation (USEF) rule book. In cases where a breed lacks a similar division, it will be left out.

Most of the breed handbooks are a wonderful compact size and are easy to navigate. Each breed has its own little differences for each of the classes, so the descriptions here are very generalized. The AQHA and APHA are the most similar. The POAs naturally are mostly geared to youth due to the pony's size, while Appaloosas also have a Saddle Seat division. Arabians have wonderful costume classes that are not covered here. Once you've been to a few horse shows, you'll know what you are looking for in the rule book; you will become more and more familiar with the information until you are an expert Horse Show Parent.

CLOTHES (AND TACK)

No other equestrian sport requires such an investment of time and money in the clothing required for even one show. If your child will do both Western and English classes, Western classes require Western tack and Western clothes, and English classes require English tack and English clothes.

Although one set of English clothes is enough, one set of Western clothes will not cut it. Western clothes (and tack) share one motto: Sparkle is good. You will need to either spend lots of money, find a good resale outlet for Western clothes, or learn to sew.

To deal with the wide variety of Western outfits required, you will also need your trainer's advice or some help from other, more experienced horse show moms. Western styles are driven by current trends seen in the breed magazines. For Showmanship classes, what your child wears should be pretty, but more importantly, well fitting. As your child progresses, you will become very savvy indeed as to the types of outfits that show off her abilities to their best advantage. For example, if your child has busy hands in a Showmanship class, you would not want to accent that with light gloves against a dark shirt.

At every horse show, most kids have different outfits for each class. And does this come to be expensive? You bet. You'll consider yourself lucky if you have only sons showing, as their clothes will require less variety and therefore less money.

The Basic Western Outfit:

1. *The hat:* The foundation of every outfit, the cowboy hat is the defining symbol of the sport. Made of felt or straw, the shapes change slightly over the years as the styles change. Straw is a good basic beginner's hat, and excellent for summer. Felt hats come in different colors. Savvy moms know that the fit and shape and color should enhance both the rider's face and attire.

2. *The belt:* A Western belt with a buckle is the standard. The more coveted belts are the ones with buckles that were earned while showing (particularly the World Buckles, which you will read about later in this chapter on pages 103–105).

3. *Boots:* Cowboy boots for both boys and girls. You may need more than one pair, depending on the class and the competition. (Although no regulation requires it, at the large regional or national shows you will see matching boots and pants in Showmanship classes.)

4. *Pants:* Depending on the class: jeans or pants, often worn under chaps.

5. *Tack:* It is important in the beginning not to make expensive investments that may be big mistakes. Selecting a saddle suitable to the job your child is trying to do should be done with your trainer's assistance. Used saddles and headstalls are available everywhere, and until your child is competing at high levels, a good serviceable saddle with some nice, showy silver will be just fine as long as it fits her and her horse.

THE GENDER GAP

Boys: Western attire for boys is relatively simple. You will need a simple assortment of clean and starched, long-sleeved Western shirts and jeans. Small Western ties in different colors, a hat, and a pair of chaps will complete the look.

Girls: Girls can require several changes of outfits for the different Western classes.

1. *Showmanship:* Pants with matching jacket top. This jacket is fitted; more like a tunic with a collar, but can be long (over the hip) or short

Showmanship with Shannon Paxton (photo by K. C. Montgomery).

Sylvia Murray ready to show.

(just to the hip). Moms usually pick the length by how it looks on their child. The colors of tops and bottoms generally match, or at least coordinate. Since this is Showmanship, the outfits are usually eye-catching, with many decorative effects. The point here is to be noticed, and for the right reasons. Glove color usually matches the sleeve of the jacket, and boots match the pants.

2. *Horsemanship and other performance classes:* Western shirt (always long-sleeved), hat, boots, and pants or jeans with optional chaps. Pants are always belted. The outfits are color-coordinated in some way, with chaps usually matching the pants.

Note: In most upper-level competition, competitors usually wear hats that go with the outfits, such as a light-colored hat for light outfits, or a black hat for darker outfits.

English outfit (photo by K.C. Montgomery).

The Basic English Outfit:

1. *Hunt coat:* a traditional hunt coat is a single-breasted jacket with back vents. It's usually a dark color, although the hunter/jumper people have been going lighter and lighter in the last several years.

2. *A "ratcatcher" shirt:* A very odd name for a button-down shirt with a detachable collar.

3. *Breeches or jodhpurs, tan in color:* The type depends on the type of boots worn with them.

4. *Paddock boots:* short-laced or zip-up English-style boots worn by younger competitors. They are worn with jodhpur (cuffed) riding pants.

5. *Tall boots:* Black, either with laces at the front of the ankle (called field boots) or dress boots (no laces). These are worn with breeches.

6. *English-style gloves:* Gloves are recommended but not required. A dark color is the norm.

7. *Tack:* Your child will need an English-type saddle and bridle, and your trainer should help you here with your choices. There is no need to purchase these items new when your child is just starting out. Your trainer may even be able to find some loaner equipment for you, to see if your child even wants to do this division.

8. *Helmet:* A hard hat in black, navy, or brown for flat classes. In all over fences classes, the helmet must be an ASTM approved helmet with a chin harness. Hair must be tucked under a hairnet (for girls).

THE EVENTS

The events (or classes) at the breed shows can be organized into three categories:

1. The horse is being judged.
2. The rider is being judged.
3. Speed (or timed) event.

All of the events listed below have a reference to each of the breed rules. Each event may be divided into age categories, such as eleven and under, twelve to fourteen, and fifteen to eighteen.

JUDGING THE HORSE

HALTER

This class will be held for a variety of horses based on age and breed. The horse is shown, as it says, at halter, meaning it is led into the arena wearing a halter and a lead rope. The judge is judging the *horse*, not your child. The basic criteria are:

1. *Conformation* of the horse. That is, how well the horse is physically put together according to the ideal of its breed. The horse stands squarely on all four feet while the judge looks him over.

Sylvia Murray and pony at halter.

2. *Soundness.* That is, not lame (limping, or otherwise traveling in an impaired fashion).

3. *"Way of travel."* The judge observes and evaluates the horse moving to and from him at a walk and a jog-trot that may travel around a corner. The judge is looking for a steady, alert, and straight four-beat natural walk and a smooth, two-beat ground-covering jog.

Although your child's horse is the one under scrutiny and will technically receive any points or prizes, her ability to get her horse into the ring and execute the required test is imperative.

Rule Book Reference: AQHA Rule 448, APHA Rule YP-085, ApHC Rule 713, POAC Rule 92, PtHA Rule 65, Arabian USEF Rule XVI, Article 1607

WESTERN RIDING

This class judges the horse for smoothness and quality of gaits, manners, and disposition as the horse and rider maneuver a pattern defined by poles and markers. There are four patterns that the judge can choose from. Each part of the pattern requires a different gait, in addition to lead changes at the lope. The total possible score is 100, with 70 considered average. Points will be added or subtracted for each maneuver based on performance. The range is +1.5 (excellent) to -1.5 (extremely poor). This is a good rule to become familiar with. It seems complicated at first, but as you gain experience, you will have a lot of fun trying to catch the errors and second-guess the judge.

Rule Book Reference: AQHA Rule 453, APHA Rule SC-255, ApHC Rule 717, POAC Rule 114, PtHA Rule 66.I, Arabian USEF Rule XVI Article 1692 (also, Rule XXXIX, Chapter V)

REINING

Very popular, and now an international discipline, reining also has its own organization, the National Reining Horse Association (NRHA), but nearly every breed show has a reining class. There is no creature so supple and light on its feet as the reining horse. Sliding to a halt in a cloud of dust, the reining horse is quickly becoming the ultimate Western horse, as much as the dressage horse is considered by some to be the classic English horse. There are several possible reining patterns, each discipline seeming to have its own variations; the pattern to be ridden is posted ahead of time.

The scoring is based on points from 1 to 100. As in Western Riding, 70 is considered an average score. Points are based on the individual maneuvers and scored in ½ point increments, from -1.5 to +1.5. A score of 0 denotes a neutral score, meaning the maneuver was done, but with no added difficulty. There is a laundry list of disqualifiers, ranging from incorrect or forbidden tack to disrespectful behavior on the part of the exhibitor. Again, your rule book is the bible here. Each discipline may have some small variations, and the NRHA has the first and last word on the sport.

Rule Book Reference: AQHA Rule 451, APHA Rule SC-125, ApHC Rule 716, POAC Rule 115, PtHA Rule 66.H, Arabian USEF Rule XVI, Article 1687

WESTERN PLEASURE

This class is similar to the Western Riding class, in that the judge is looking for smoothness of gaits, nice transitions, and an easy, balanced way of going. The horse should be a pleasure to ride and in good fit condition. Unlike the Western Riding class, there is no pattern, but the judge does want to see the horse go both directions at a walk, jog, and lope. He may also ask for an extended walk, jog, or lope.

Rule Book Reference: AQHA Rule 463, APHA Rule SC-245, ApHC Rule 718, POAC Rule 112, PtHA Rule 66.D, Arabian USEF Rule XVI, Chapter XIX, Article 1681

TRAIL

Each discipline has its own rules, but the object is the same: to simulate obstacles that would normally be found on a trail ride, and test the horse's ability to maneuver such obstacles. The horse is being judged on how he maneuvers the obstacles, which include a gate that riders open, pass through, and close. Horse and rider must also ride over at least four logs (AQHA), and depending on the class, these may be elevated, even to a level that needs to be jumped. A backing obstacle is also required, such as backing through and around markers arranged in the shape of a T or an L. You may see serpentine obstacles, water hazards (small ditch or pond), and a wooden bridge to walk over. Riders may be required to carry something from one part of the arena to the other, put on a slicker and remove it, and take a letter out of a mailbox. Horses should be willing and pleasant as they maneuver the obstacles. Points are given or taken away for each movement, then totaled for an overall score. Sometimes reverse scoring is used for this class, with the lowest score coming out the winner. Rules in specific are given in each breed's rule book.

Rule Book Reference: AQHA Rule 454, APHA Rule SC-250, ApHC Rule 724, POAC Rule 113, PtHA Rule 66.E, Arabian USEF Rule XVI, Article 1690

HUNTER UNDER SADDLE

"Under Saddle" means that the horse is shown with a mounted rider, not at halter. The way of going, conformation, willingness, and performance are the elements used for judging. Your child will be asked to walk/trot/and canter on the rail. A typical "hunter," according to the AQHA rule book (Rule 464.a) should "move with long, low strides reaching forward with ease and smoothness." They should also be able to "lengthen stride and cover ground with relaxed, free-flowing movement." In addition, the "poll should be level with, or slightly above, the withers," and have a "bright expression with alert ears, and should respond willingly to the rider with light leg and hand contact."

Rule Book Reference: AQHA Rule 464, APHA Rule SC-205, ApHC Rule 772, POAC Rule 117, PtHA Rule 68.C, Arabian USEF Rule XVI, Chapter VII, Article 1641

U

The Horse Show Mom: Don't expect to "get" this right away. It takes many horse shows, and sometimes years (as in my case) to really see what the judge is looking for. In a class of ten horses, if nine were high-stepping Saddlebreds, and your daughter was riding her easygoing Quarter Horse, chances are she'd be the winner. It's quite hard for me to imagine anything so simple ever taking place. The more likely scenario is one similar to this: There will be a nice hunter type which would normally place ahead of the other horses, but today goes with its ears pinned back and pulling its rider out of the saddle, and as a result, the slightly more upright-moving horse gets the goods (ribbon).

Some judges have their own preferences for a hunter type, and since this is a subjective class, you'll just have to get used to the idea that the show ring can be a less than perfect world. From my many years of experience, I can say only that what goes around, comes around. One show, the judge will miss the horse that stopped for a moment. You may be irate if the child is pinned ahead of yours. But at the next show, it may be your child's horse that stops, and you'll be happy to see that the judge missed that one, too. Imagine yourself in the arena trying to judge twenty horses at once.

HUNTER OVER FENCES (OR WORKING HUNTER)

The horse is shown over a minimum of eight fences, and each round must include a change of direction. The hunter/jumper section of this book is a good reference for the type of jumps used (in the H/J glossary, page 112) and how the class is judged. The minimum height for youth classes is 3 feet with a maximum of 3'3" except for novice, which will be 2'6" to a high of 3'.

Rule Book Reference: AQHA Rule 460, APHA Rule 215, ApHC Rule 775, POAC Rule 119, PtHA Rule 68.D, Arabian USEF Rule XVI, Chapter IX, Article 1641

HUNTER HACK

In hunter/jumper world, "hack" refers to a flat class. In Western world, a hunter hack is a type of hunter horse, and the class includes jumping and a flat phase. The horse is first required to jump two fences, at a height of 2'3" to 3'. If the jumps go well, horse and rider could be called back for a flat phase of walk, trot, and canter. There may be other tests asked by the judge when appropriate, such as a hand gallop, halt, or back-up. The judge is looking for way of going, manners, and style, and the outcome is based on 70 percent for the jumping work and 30 percent on the flat.

Rule Book Reference: AQHA Rule 462, APHA Rule SC-210, ApHC Rule 778, POAC Rule 120, PtHA Rule 68.H, Arabian USEF Rule XVI, Chapter IX, Article 1641

JUDGING THE RIDER/HANDLER

SHOWMANSHIP AT HALTER

Each breed has its own rules and judging criteria, but basics are that the horse should be well groomed, and hooves should be clean and correctly trimmed or shod, with clean, well-fitting, and appropriate tack. Your child should be dressed neatly in the appropriate Western attire, and perform the task with confidence and poise. Her task includes leading the horse from its left side, while holding the lead rope in the right hand. Her right hand should be near the halter, while her left hand holds the remaining lead shank. Your child will halt, back, turn her horse around, and set him up squarely, according to the rules for this class and each horse show. She should be at a safe distance for correct handling, will not be allowed to touch her horse during the process, and should not block the judge's view of her horse by standing between the judge and her horse.

Minor faults would include performing the correct maneuvers, but not always at the designated marker; giving too many verbal cues; failure to have the horse squarely set up, or taking too long to set him up; and having a horse not groomed to show standards.

Major faults would be given for completely obstructing the judge's view; knocking over or working on the wrong side of a cone; failure to complete some of the maneuvers, or adding others not asked for; pointing her feet at the horse's hooves during set up (a disallowed way to cue a horse to stand squarely); touching her horse; and standing directly in front of her horse.

Disqualifications are given if her horse gets away from her, if she doesn't have a number, if she leads on the wrong side, if she abuses her horse, or if her horse behaves in any manner that could be unsafe for her or the other exhibitors (kicking, biting, etc.).

Rule Book Reference: AQHA Rule 471, APHA Rule YP-100, ApHC Rule 791, POAC Rule 111, PtHA Rule 86, Arabian USEF Rule XVI, Chapter XXIII, Article 1699

---— **U** ---—

The Horse Show Mom: Now the judge is judging your child. It's easy to be confused, but the most important thing to remember is that if you have a horse with unfortunate conformation—that is, not the prettiest thing in the arena—your child is still on an even footing with all the other kids. If her horse is impeccably turned out, with a sparkling coat, clean and correct tack, your child is in her best show attire, and her horse is a willing and obedient partner, she has a chance to be the winner. Even the horse with the most expensive pedigree will not win if his owner lacks the skills for this class.

WESTERN HORSEMANSHIP

This class tests the rider's control. It may be that your child performs in an arena with other exhibitors, or individually, "from the gate." The judge posts the pattern for performance at the beginning of the show day, but not less than an hour before the class, although he may ask for additional patterns once the group or individual is in the arena. The exhibitors can be asked to walk, trot, lope along the rail; make circles, figure eights, or serpentine figures; perform a halt and rein-back, flying changes, counter-canter; ride without stirrups; or other movements, depending upon the level of the class. The judge might use a point system (e.g., twenty points, with ten going to rider's appearance and position as well as her horse's appearance, and ten to the execution of the required performance). Even though the rider is primarily the one being judged, her horse's unruliness can count against her. Again, each breed has its own rule book, and parents should familiarize themselves with their breed's performance and judging criteria.

Rule Book Reference: AQHA Rule 472, APHA Rule YP-120, ApHC Rule 796, PtHA Rule 87B (see Stock Seat Equitation), Arabian USEF Rule XVI, Chapter XXII, Article 1699

Shannon Paxton in horsemanship attire (photo by K.C. Montgomery).

HUNT SEAT EQUITATION

This class requires English tack and attire and is performed at the walk, trot, and canter. Like Western Horsemanship, it has a required pattern that will be posted ahead of the class time. The patterns will include trot and canter, and depending on the level, may require a sitting and posting trot, extended and collected trots, canter, counter-canter, leg yields, flying changes, and turn on the forehand, in addition to performing these through figure eights, serpentines, and other patterns. Judging, as in horsemanship, is based on the rider's position, correctness of the aids, and execution of the gaits and patterns.

HUNT SEAT EQUITATION OVER FENCES

The fence heights are 2'6" to 3'. There will be at least six fences to jump, and the class is judged similarly to the flat class with regard to the rider's position and ability.

Rule Book Reference: AQHA Rules 473 & 474, APHA Rule YP-115, ApHC Rule 797, POAC Rules 109–110, PtHA Rule 87.C, Arabian USEF Rule XVI, Chapter XXI, Article 1694

LEADLINE

For the little cowboys and cowgirls, ages three to eight, this class will probably get you into the show ring, too. Your child may not be eligible to ride in any other class at a particular show if she enters the Leadline class, but her horse or pony is free to enter other classes with a different rider. The tack and attire may be English or Western, but not a mix of both. (For

Leadline with Marylynn Murray and daughter Jacque.

example, she can't wear Western clothes and ride in an English saddle.) Anyone eighteen years or older can lead the child, but usually it's you, Mom. The child's feet must be correctly in the stirrups and she must have some equitation ability. The leader will hold the lead shank, but the performance is up to the pilot in the saddle. If the judge asks her to back up, she must get her pony to back up without your help. If you love to dress up, here's your chance to please the spectators.

Rule Book Reference: APHA Rule YP-105, ApHC Rule 793, POAC Rule 106, PtHA Rule 82.K

SPEED EVENTS

BARRELS

Barrels are brightly colored 55-gallon drums, set in a cloverleaf pattern at specified distances. The rider gets a running start across the starting line's timers, then proceeds to the number-one barrel and makes a 360-degree turn around it, and then moves across to the next barrel, and so on, until she has completed the course. She then sprints back across the finish line. There is a specified direction for each 360-degree turn, with a change of direction for each barrel. A barrel that is knocked over acquires a five-second penalty, added to the total elapsed time. Any missed barrels, or deviation from the pattern, results in elimination.

Rule Book Reference: AQHA Rule 456, APHA Rule SC-290, ApHC Rule 729, POAC Rules 126 & 127, PtHA Rule 74.C, Arabian USEF Rule XVI, Chapter XXV, Article 1699S

POLE BENDING

Pole bending is a fun obstacle race where the rider is timed from the starting line and must "bend" her horse around the six-pole course, changing direction for each one, much like a slalom. Missing a pole or going off course gets one eliminated, but knocking down a pole only acquires a time penalty of five seconds. The fastest time wins.

Rule Book Reference: AQHA Rule 457, APHA Rule SC-295, ApHC Rule 730, POAC Rule 125, PtHA Rule 74.D, Arabian USEF Rule XVI, Chapter XXV, Article 1699R

OPEN JUMPING

Jumping is a timed event with the winner completely determined by clear rounds (with no rails lowered), no refusals, and in the case of equality of faults, time. If, in a class of eight, the slowest rider is the only one who went clear (meaning no rails knocked down, and no refusals), then that rider is the winner. Riders are usually required to jump at least eight obstacles set from 18" for young POA riders to 3'6" in some of the higher divisions. English attire is required.

Rule Book Reference: AQHA Rule 459, APHA Rule SC-220, ApHC Rule 773, POAC Rule 118, PtHA Rule 68.F, Arabian USEF Rule XVI, Chapter X, Article 1648

THE POINTS: TIME TO ADD 'EM UP

Understanding the lingo, the classes, and the judging is the big preparation for every horse show parent's real goal: winning! This, of course, is tongue in cheek, but lest we get too holy about it, most parents like to know what the points mean, how they are won, and where they will take their child in her show career. The information given here and in Appendix I A through F (pages 197–215) is a general guideline. You will need to check your breed's handbook, which by now should be more or less permanently attached to you. Each horse show, each state, and each zone will have its own spin on the points, but if you understand the basic way they are laid out, you will become quickly proficient with all the other nuances.

The Ribbons

Ribbons are awarded for each place, with some breeds giving ribbons through sixth place and others through eighth place.

1st Blue Ribbon

2nd Red

3rd Yellow

4th White

5th Pink

6th Green

7th Purple

8th Brown

Ribbons and buckles.

While ribbons are popular with kids, the bigger prizes of trophies and belt buckles have much more allure. The colors are consistent throughout the horse world.

For all of the breeds, except the Arabian, the following holds true: Points earned in each class go to two things—a high-point overall award for each age division, and national points for year-end awards and cumulative honors. Zone or area points are also earned, and go to year-end recognition awards for each zone.

Points are earned based on the number of competitors in a particular class, and may also be based on the number of judges at the horse show. There can be many classes at a horse show, and your child might show in several throughout the day (or days), depending on the show. Your child will always show in only one age division at any given show.

Each breed has its own point calculations. To skip right to your breed's point information, go to the following appendices: AQHA (Appendix I A, page 197), APHA (Appendix I B, page 201), ApHC (Appendix I C, page 205), POAC (Appendix I D, page 207), PtHA (Appendix I E, page 211), and AHA (Appendix I F, page 215).

THE BIG SHOWS

Big national shows and finals exist in nearly every equestrian sport. For competitive kids, these are the goals of the year. Most every discipline has a zone or regional final of some sort, plus a national-level final that includes the best competition in the country. Below are the major Western breed shows of this type.

AMERICAN QUARTER HORSE ASSOCIATION (AQHA)

AQHA Youth World Show: Held in Fort Worth every August, the World Youth Show is the annual goal for competitive youth riders, and winning a World Buckle at that event is the ultimate experience in a young rider's career. Qualifying points (from May 1 to April 30) are necessary; the list can be found in Appendix I A on page 197.

All American Quarter Horse Congress: Another big annual show is the All American Quarter Horse Congress. Held in Columbus, Ohio, every

October, it is open to any rider wishing to enter. Your child can expect to compete against over one hundred of the best in the nation.

AMERICAN PAINT HORSE ASSOCIATION (APHA)

Paint-O-Ramas: These are big shows where there are multiple judges in the ring (up to four) and as such give competitors multiple points. Plus, the prizes here are great. Watches, saddles, and televisions are a few of the possible prizes for the winners at Paint-O-Ramas. Some special rules about these shows are covered in Rule SC-105.

Zone-O-Ramas: This is a zone show that also has multiple judges, up to a limit of six on two or more days. Also covered in Rule SC-105.

Paint World: Like the AQHA's Youth World Show, Paint World is the big one of the year for APHA. Held every year in late June at the Will Rogers Center in Fort Worth, Texas, most of the youth classes will have over one hundred entries each. The World Show is the style setter for the coming year, so many parents and kids enjoy watching these, even if they are not competing. Next year's aspiring winners will be on the lookout for the new trends. Every keen competitor has set their sights on this one. A World Buckle is a treasure.

APPALOOSA HORSE CLUB (APHC)

World Champion Appaloosa Youth Horse Show: The big Appaloosa youth event of the year is held in late June through early July in Oklahoma City. Youths may enter as long as they are members, and have owned their horse for at least thirty days prior to the show. In practical terms, this means that the horse must be properly registered with ApHC thirty days before the show.

PONY OF THE AMERICAS CLUB (POAC)

There are several important POAC shows every year: the Regional Shows, the Eastern and Western Classic, and the International Show. These shows are all more exciting than any local show, and all give extra points to those who place. The Regional Shows give awards to eight places, and International Shows pin to ten places, in addition to lots of special awards. These shows are the goal of every competitive pony rider in the POAC. The shows are exciting and fun, and can be a great event for the whole family (POAC Rules 65–70).

The International Show: The pinnacle show for the POAC each year, it is generally held in the same place for two or three years before moving to another location. All locations are in the central part of the country, in states like Oklahoma, Michigan, and Missouri.

PINTO HORSE ASSOCIATION OF AMERICA (PTHA)

Multi-Judge Shows: Shows that are multi-judged are basically considered separate shows running at the same time. For practical purposes, your child will compete in a class with two judges and receive two separate results and scores.

Area Championship Shows: Each area can run one of these shows per year. There is one judge, but the points are tripled.

World Champion Pinto Horse Show: This is the big event for the year. There are more points awarded, and the big goal, of course, is to be World Champion in your best division, and go home with one of those wonderful World Buckles! Riders earn a set of points from each judge and a set of overall points.

ARABIAN HORSE ASSOCIATION (AHA)

Regional Shows: There are thirteen national Regionals in the AHA. They are held in June and July every year, prior to the national show. The top five in each division at Regionals qualify for the National Show.

Annual Youth Arabian and Half-Arabian Championship Horse Show: This show is held in Albuquerque, New Mexico, in late July of every year, and is the goal for those young riders wishing to be at the top of their sport. Champions win highly prized horse statue trophies and leather jackets.

Canadian National Arabian and Half-Arabian Championship Horse Show: Held every year in late August, the Canadian National Show is open to adults and youth from the United States and Canada. The same qualifications for the U.S. Youth Nationals hold for the Canadian show. It is held in Regina, Saskatchewan.

YEAR-END AWARDS
AMERICAN QUARTER HORSE ASSOCIATION
All year-end and cumulative awards are based on a one horse/one rider combination.

High-Point Horse (Rule 4313A): An AQHA trophy is awarded to the youth horse/rider combination who has earned the most points in a particular event for the year. That is, if your child has the most points in Western Pleasure, she will win the High-Point Award for that event.

All-Around High-Point Horse (Rule 432): A High-Point and Reserve (second place) will be awarded to the youth who has accumulated the most combined overall points nationwide in Halter and at least two performance categories. At least five points must be earned in each category, adding up to the grand total.

AMERICAN PAINT HORSE ASSOCIATION
There are two types of year-end awards: one for the horse, and one for the rider. Every award is counted only as a horse and rider combination. That is, whichever horse your daughter rides, those points go to that combination alone. Your daughter may win an equitation class at ten different horse shows, but if she competes on different horses, it will dilute her points for a year-end championship.

The APHA gives year-end awards for high-point winners for each division (age), and for the horse.

———————————— U ————————————

The Horse Show Mom: As an example, we will use two make-believe competitors, Jack and Jill, who both compete in the thirteen-and-under classes. Jack owns two horses: Dusty and Springfield. Jill owns one horse: Elvis. Jack competes in the following classes on Dusty: Youth Western Pleasure, Youth Horsemanship, and Youth Trail. He competes in the following classes on Springfield: Youth Showmanship, Youth Hunter under Saddle, and Youth Hunt Seat Equitation. Jack is a fine competitor and usually gets points at most horse shows, but not for every class. His hunter type horse, Springfield, does particularly well in the Hunter classes, and he wins the national high-point award for the year.

Jill competes in the following classes on Elvis: Youth Showmanship, Youth Western Pleasure, Youth Horsemanship, Youth Trail, Youth Hunter, Youth Hunt Seat Equitation, plus occasionally, a Barrels class. Jill does well enough to get points in most classes at every horse show, so much so that she and her horse are zone high-point winners in the Trail class, and overall national high-point winners because she goes to a lot of shows. Since she and Elvis are partners for so many different classes, they accrue the most points.

APHA Youth Top Twenty Award: This award goes to the top twenty point earners in Youth halter and performance classes. A maximum of twenty shows are used, all of which must be APHA approved and must have been judged by twenty different judges. Buckles are awarded to the top twenty in each age group (Rule YP-055).

APHA Youth Honor Roll Award: The horse/rider combination earning the most points in each event during the calendar year is awarded this title. (A minimum of six points must be earned.) The award is given for each age group. Those placing second through tenth for the year will receive certificates (Rule YP-060).

APHA Youth Zone Award: This award is given to the top five youth in each of the APHA zones. The points earned for this award must be earned in the competitor's home zone (Rule YP-065).

APPALOOSA HORSE CLUB

Annual High-Point Youth Award: This is earned in each class and under each age division listed under Rule 803. The youth may earn points on more than one horse, but *must* earn at least five points in that particular event. If there are ties, both competitors receive the award.

Annual Youth Versatility Award: This is a one horse/one rider award given to the high-point youth in each age division. The competitor must have earned points in Showmanship and Performance, with at least five points in one division, on the same horse throughout the year (Rule 803).

PONY OF THE AMERICAS CLUB

For all the points earned during a show, the accumulated effort goes toward a national recognition at the end of the year. There are many different awards based on the high-point winners in each division, or an overall top ten for all of the divisions. Rule 141 in the POAC handbook lists all of these awards and their descriptions.

High-Point Pony Award: Given to a pony, not the rider (although obviously, the owner gets to enjoy this prize). For all approved classes, points will accumulate throughout the year. The pony can be ridden by different riders. However, if the pony is ridden in the same type of class but in different age divisions, only one rider can be designated for points. This designation must be made prior to the class, or no points will be given.

High-Point Rider Award: This allows a pony rider to accumulate points on different ponies. However, if your child rides two ponies in one division, only one set of those points will count. You must make the designation prior to the start of the class.

High-Point Showmanship and Equitation Award: Overall high points accumulated in any approved POAC Showmanship and Equitation classes, judged on the rider.

One Pony/One Rider Award: For all approved POAC classes, (whether halter, showmanship, equitation or performance classes), for a pony and rider combination.

Medallions (Rule 149): Medallions are awarded to riders who win one hundred points in a year in a particular division. A nominating fee must first be paid before the points begin to accumulate. Once your young rider is proficient in a particular area, this is a good one to go for.

PINTO HORSE ASSOCIATION

As in the other breed disciplines, year-end awards are offered to horse and rider combinations and to the horses themselves. These awards are offered in two age groups: thirteen and under, and fourteen to eighteen.

NATIONAL ˙

Top Ten Youth of the Year: For each event, the top ten in each age group are recognized for their achievement. The rider in the number-one spot receives a beautiful buckle.

High-Point: A year-end high-point award goes to the rider with the most points overall. For example: A twelve-year-old rider who accumulates the most points in the nation in all of the ROM point classes would win High-Point Youth Award.

ZONE

In addition to the national awards, each of the seven zones offers the following year-end award:

Overall High Point: The top five from each zone across the United States and Canada are recognized.

ARABIAN HORSE ASSOCIATION

Arabian horses can qualify for a variety of year-end awards, both from the Arabian Horse Association and the United States Equestrian Federation. One popular year-end award for youth is the Regional Youth Team Tournament. Each member organization (such as your state organization) designates teams. While each rider competes individually, the team accumulates points over the year for a set of classes that they chose at the beginning of the year. For example, the team may decide to accumulate points in Trail, Western Horsemanship, and Showmanship. These points are tallied, and team winners are named at the end of the year.

The Youth of the Year is awarded by the AHA to one young rider per year, based on nominations submitted. The winner is chosen by committee.

The Horse of the Year Award (HOTYA) is awarded regionally and nationally by the USEF for the overall high points for Western Pleasure and Hunter Pleasure horse ridden by a junior exhibitor.

Grand Champion Arabian and Half/Anglo-Arabian Junior Exhibitor's Horse Awards are given to each junior with the highest total points for all classes entered. Point values are based on placing and number of competitors in each division at horse shows throughout the year. The information for these awards is available in the awards section of the United States Equestrian Federation rule book, available online at www.usef.org.

WESTERN RESOURCES
Web Sites
www.apha.com: The American Paint Horse Association (APHA) hosts a Web site with membership details, breed information, rules, and more.

www.appaloosa.com: The Appaloosa Horse Club (AHC) Web site and information center.

www.aqha.com: The American Quarter Horse Association (AQHA) Web site, with information about competitions, rules, clinics, and other events.

www.arabianhorses.org: The Arabian Horse Association (AHA) Web site. Rules, competitions, results, youth events, and more are covered.

www.equisearch.com: Primedia, Inc. (publisher of *Horse & Rider* and *Equus*) Web site with articles, news, and links for all horse disciplines.

www.pinto.org: The Pinto Horse Association of America (PtHA) Web site, with rules, membership, and information.

www.poac.org: The Pony of the Americas Club (POAC) Web site.

Publications
Equus Magazine: another Primedia publication covering general areas of interest for horse lovers.

Horse & Rider Magazine: Subtitled "The Authority on Western Riding and Training," this magazine (published by Primedia, Inc.) covers a broad range of subjects for the Western horseperson.

Western Horsemanship by Richard Shrake, published by Western Horseman, takes a simple and well-thought-out approach to the basics of Western riding. This book has loads of pictures and is a great handy reference.

In addition, breed and activity organizations have their own membership publications.

Hunter/Jumpers and Equitation

Evolving out of the hunt field, this discipline is both popular and fiercely competitive. Although its ranks include diverse incomes and background, its image of hunt coats, breeches, fine boots, and elegant saddles and tack give the subliminal message of leisure and disposable income. It attracts thousands of young pony riders who go on to become polished riders in what is referred to as their "junior career," until the age of eighteen. In fact, there are over 16,000 USEF members competing in this beautiful English-style sport. Called hunter/jumpers, the sport actually encompasses three disciplines which have obvious similarities, but subtle and unique differences.

Show jumping is an Olympic sport: exciting, breathtaking, and at the higher levels, for the most courageous and talented horses and riders. Equitation grew out of a need to make our riders better competitors in the international arena. It began in the '50s, and has encouraged our present young riders to emulate what is known as the beautiful "American style." Originally a "function follows form" idea, equitation (or "horsemanship") has now become somewhat of an end in itself, with the year-end Equitation finals being the dream and goal of any self-respecting young hunt seat rider. "Hunters" is a discipline that encourages fine breeding of beautiful and talented horses, and while the rider is a necessary and important element, the horse is the one being judged.

At top-rated hunter/jumper shows, you may see tack rooms decorated more elegantly than your living room. Horses may wear "coolers" that cost more than your winter coat (and "cooler" doesn't mean it keeps him cool). So here are a few terms from this highly nuanced discipline to get you started, and also to give you a leg up on the rest of this chapter. A more complete glossary is at the back of the book (beginning on page 243).

FIRST THINGS FIRST: A BEGINNER'S HUNTER/JUMPER GLOSSARY

Canter: A controlled gallop, with the foreleg to the inside of the arena or working area leading ahead of the other legs when the horse is on the correct lead.

Champion: The winner of a division. This is determined by adding the number of points the rider earns in each class of her division. See the ribbons on page 142 and the corresponding points.

Change of lead: When changing direction at the canter, the horse balances himself by changing the leading leg. This can be done by walking or trotting through the change; when it's done instantly, it's called a flying change.

Chip: Not a food or a desired commodity, but plentiful nonetheless, when the horse or pony plants a big out-of-sync step or "stride" right in front of the jump. For example, if your child is supposed to count and ride five strides between two jumps in a line, but instead of five even strides, the horse fits in an awkward extra stride, it's called a chip.

Cooler: A wool blanket, often with fancy braided trim, for your child's pony/horse to wear to and from the ring. It can come in your barn's colors, and you can have the pony's name professionally embroidered on it.

Exhibitor: A horse show participant. (This counts for moms too, so don't let the parking attendant charge you to get in.)

Fences: The obstacles to be jumped.[1] There are many different styles of obstacle fences, all with their own names. In hunters, the fences are meant

---

[1] The fence that goes around the outside and defines the perimeter of the arena is actually called the rail, and the open area where your child goes through is the gate. Sometimes there is an actual gate that is opened and closed; other times it's merely virtual. The in-gate is where your child waits to go "in" and where her trainer normally stands during your child's round.

Hunter/Jumper exhibitor at the rail.

to simulate those natural obstacles that would be found in the hunting field. Here's the fence glossary:

- *Aiken:* Brush on *two* sides with a rail on top. The name originated in Aiken, South Carolina.
- *Brush:* Natural brush at the base of a jump, or sometimes all by itself.
- *Combination:* Either two or three jumps in a row, with one or two strides in between jumps.
- *Coop:* This is a triangular jump that is supposed to resemble a chicken coop. (No chickens, though.)
- *Fan:* A fence that fans out on one side.
- *Gate:* Resembles a gate, if only vaguely.
- *Hog's back:* A triple oxer, three elements together with the middle being the highest. Imagination helps.
- *In-and-Out:* One of the few names that make sense. Two jumps in a row, pony/horse to jump in, land, take one or two strides, jump out. The strides in between are specific to each course; a one stride should not be done in two strides.
- *Liverpool:* A water jump, typically a blue mat on the ground adjacent to the fence that occasionally has water in it. At the Grand Prix

The fan.

Hog's back.

jumping level (you're a long way from that), it may actually be a small pool in the ground, and very wide at that.

- *Oxer:* This is basically two jumps close together, to be jumped as one. The spread (distance between the two elements) is related to the height of the jump. The higher the jumps, the wider the spread. The name actually does refer to oxen, which, although they can jump fences, are reluctant to do so if the fences are wide. Pasture fences for cows and oxen are often doubled for this reason.
- *Stone wall:* Just what it says, except it's a painted wooden box. Mediocre trompe l'oeil.

The liverpool.

The oxer.

- *Swedish oxer:* Poles are set at an angle to each other on the opposite standards.
- *Triple bar:* Three rails with ascending heights, front to back.
- *Vertical:* A single fence without width except for the rails.
- *Wings:* The ends on either end of a jump. They give the jump a more solid look. A more difficult jump is one without these wings.

The Swedish oxer.

The triple bar.

The vertical.

Hands: Did you know that you had an equine measuring device attached to your arm? Based on an approximation of a big man's fist (four inches across the back), all ponies and horses are measured in a combination of "hands" and "inches." A 13.1 hand pony is 53" tall. The measurement is taken from the floor to the highest point of the pony's withers.

Jog: Before ribbons are awarded in hunter classes, the judge asks for the horses to "jog" or be led into the arena at a trot to check for soundness. Horses found to be unsound or lame will not be awarded a ribbon.

Lead: The way in which the horse properly balances himself at the canter. When going to the left, the left foreleg (inside leg) leads the other foreleg.

On the flat: Usually an equitation class, riders perform at the walk, trot, and canter with no obstacles to be jumped.

Pin, pinning, pinned: A ribbon, getting a ribbon, having gotten a ribbon. Not normally pinned on anything, occasionally hung from the horse's bridle, but usually handed out to the top six, eight, or ten riders, depending upon the class. Ribbon colors and point values are found on page 142.

Post: The act of rising and sitting with the horse's motion at the trot.

Prize list: The booklet that arrived before the show with an entry form and a list of classes offered. It also contains suggestions for local hotels, a map, and other useful information. Not, however, a list of key rings, saddle pads, coolers, or other cool prizes that come along with the blue ribbons. (Cash prizes for certain classes *will* be listed.)

Reserve: One spot past the last ribbon given out. In a class pinned to six, it means 7th place. In a class pinned to eight, it means 9th place.

Reserve Champion: A division's second-place winner.

Rollback turn: A 180-degree hairpin turn to a jump going the other way from the previously jumped fence.

Shadbelly: A formal coat worn in a Hunter Classic class. It comes in navy or black and is double-breasted with tails.

Soundness: Absence of lameness.

Stride: One complete horse step at the trot or canter.

Swap: This is a "changed" flying lead on the way to the jump. Horses and ponies will often do so on their own to rebalance themselves. Judges have varying opinions on this, but there are times when it results in a markdown.

Trot: A four-beat gait. The rider usually "posts" at the trot, but may be asked to "sit" the trot in an equitation class.

Wrong lead: Cantering on the incorrect lead, such as the right foreleg and hind leg preceding the left ones when the horse is cantering to the left.

USEF RULE BOOK

The United States Equestrian Federation (USEF) Rule Book, which is published online and available in printed form to members, is an essential reference for anyone, parent or child, who wishes to understand the rules and structure of this sport. The information given below and the accompanying section on points, all came from the USEF Rule Book. Any class or division that is covered by the rules includes a reference to that corresponding rule. Each class or division also has a page reference to its associated point calculator.

SOME BASIC FACTS

Your first hunter/jumper show will set you to some head-scratching confusion. Just recognizing the differences among hunters, jumpers, and equitation will take some time. First of all, most classes involve jumping. Second of all, a quick glance at the rings will show you that the hunters and equitation all look pretty much the same. In the jumpers, generally, the fences are brighter, scarier, and more plentiful than in the other rings, but a low-level jumping course may also be pretty similar to a hunter or equitation arena. There *are* real distinctions among all three types, but they will take time to learn. And as it is not unlikely that your child will compete in more than one type, you will definitely need to get out the ginkgo.

The classes your child will compete in are based on many factors. The ability to ride in a particular division is a combination of your child's riding skill and the suitability of her mount—to the fence heights, and also to the particular job. This is for your trainer to decide. It also will depend on your child's eligibility, which has to do with age, how many blue ribbons she's won, and which breed or other organizations she belongs to. To accumulate points, at all rated shows she will need to be a member of the United States Equestrian Federation (USEF) and the United States Hunter Jumper Association (USHJA). To accumulate points for year-end state awards, she will also need to be a member of your local state organization. If she competes regularly in a neighboring state, she may also need to belong to that organization as well, at least if she wants to accumulate points for their year-end awards. (These subjects will be covered as the chapter goes on and in the hunter/jumper appendix.)

Before You Begin

- Before you get to the horse show, you will be introduced to the prize list with the entry form. If you are asked by your trainer to fill it out, be sure that you have the following:

USEF Junior Membership: $35.00 per year (as of 2005)

USHJA Junior Membership: $25.00 per year (as of 2005)

Horse Recording: $75.00 per year or $200.00 Lifetime Recording

---

- Membership in other associations becomes necessary as your child moves up and begins to compete for particular year-end awards or for regional qualifiers. Save your money until then, but for reference, here are some of the organizations that you will come to know along the way: USET, Maclay, WIHS, Marshall and Sterling League, and NAL. The section on points and year-end finals will explain these in more detail. (See Appendix IIA, page 217.)
- Your trainer's USEF number and address and phone numbers.
- Your child's horse or pony's USEF number.
- If you have a pony, a copy of her measurement card. The same goes for a Junior Hunter horse. Ponies and Junior Hunter horses are shown by "size."
- Your child's social security number or a Federal ID number if her pony or horse is owned by a farm or corporation, just in case your child wins prize money. Don't count on it being enough to warrant a 1099 tax form.
- A list of the classes that your trainer wants your child to compete in.
- A magnifying glass. This is for the tiny little squares on the entry blank. The horse shows try to fit so much on one little entry blank that it seems as if they start with a poster-sized form and then shrink it down a thousand times.
- You will also need to provide proof of negative Coggins (proof that your horse does not have equine infectious anemia, a highly contagious disease), plus a current health certificate from your vet.

- A check. Or a credit card, if you dare . . . not a recommended start for a sport that becomes addictive.
- An understanding of the "age" rule: The USEF has its own view of the calendar. Its year begins on December 1 and ends on November 30. Whatever age your child is on December 1 will determine her "showing" age for the following year. For example: If your daughter turned ten on January 1, 2005, she will show as a nine-year-old until November 30 of 2005, and a ten-year-old in 2006, even though her real age will be eleven for all of that year. She will be competing (to her advantage) against others who really are ten years old, but have more unfortunate birthdays (such as this author's daughter, whose birthday falls on November 21). This "aging" thing happens in many sports, and is just the luck of the draw. (Perhaps more forward-thinking equestrian parents will try to plan their children's births around this system.)

CLOTHING

Compared to other disciplines, the hunter/jumper clothing requirements are relatively simple, if not cheap. Hunters and equitation riders wear basically the same outfits, although some riders have separate jackets. And the jumpers are not so formal, unless at a year-end final or a big "classic" class when the riders wear coats. The worst part of the investment for any parent is at the beginning, and then during those years when the child grows three boot sizes!

Pants

JODHPURS

These are long cuffed riding pants with suede or fake suede inserts on the inside of the calf. They are for the younger riders who are too small for tall boots. Trainers have varying opinions, but the smallest kids look great in jodhpurs and somewhat overwhelmed in tall boots and breeches. They come in a few shades of tan and khaki.

BREECHES

Worn with tall boots, breeches are stretchy and of varying fabrics and quality. They are form fitting and reach down to the lower calf. Riders usually wear thin, knee-high socks over the breeches and under the boot.
Hunters and Equitation: Khaki or tan are the colors.

Jumpers: Khaki or tan is fine, except for Jumper Classics when white is preferred (but not always required).

Boots
PADDOCK BOOTS
For the younger set who still wear jodhpurs, these are short leather boots that zip or tie. They are considerably cheaper than tall boots, and typically brown.

FIELD BOOTS
The tall boot of choice for hunter/jumpers, they can range from $140 to over $1,200 (if custom-made). They are black, with laces in the front part of the ankle. They can come with or without zippers up the back.

Shirts
Hunters and Equitation: Often referred to as "ratcatcher" shirts, females' hunter show shirts have a separate stand-up collar that buttons to the shirt and is typically initialed or worn with a pin. These shirts come in long- and short-sleeved, but the typical is long-sleeved. They come in white and many other colors, usually pastels, with stripes, checks, and plaids. Subtle is better.
Jumpers: Other than finals and classic classes when shirts and coats are required, most jumping classes allow polo shirts. They must have sleeves and a collar and be tucked into breeches with a belt. Solid colors are the norm, but stripes are also worn.

Jackets
Hunters and Equitation: Navy is traditionally preferred for equitation, but over the last few years the colors have been getting lighter. Hunters have gone to greens, browns, blues, and tans. Navy is good for either division. Fabric can be wool or synthetic, gabardine or other flat weave. Subtle windowpanes and pinstripes are gaining popularity.
Jumpers: Jackets are not always required, but some kids wear their jackets anyway, no matter what the color. Navy may be required for some classes; see the prize list for any particular show you are attending.

Dressed to show.

Helmets

Every junior rider who shows must wear an ASTM-approved helmet, with its under-chin harness fastened at all times while he or she is mounted, whether or not in the show ring. The helmets have evolved over the years from being very low-profile velvet hard hats to the much rounder and more protective head gear of today. ASTM is the stamp of approval for safety-tested head gear. The most popular current style is the European jumper style with a center stripe, which can be worn in the hunters, equitation, and jumpers.

Most trainers prefer to have girls tie their hair up under the helmet with a hairnet. It takes a little practice, but once you and your child learn, it can be done in a flash.

Gloves

Black or brown, usually to match the boot color. Leather or synthetic is fine. There are many synthetic stretchy fabrics for gloves that make for greater comfort, although leather is always popular.

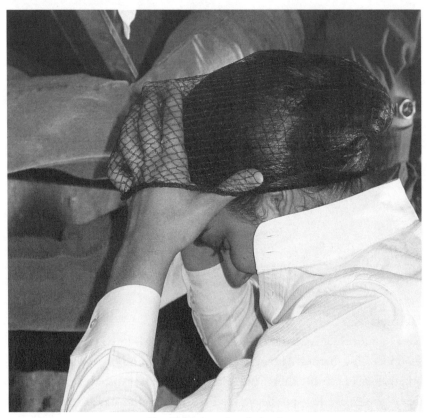

Alex May preparing helmet.

Elizabeth Glazer helping daughter Kelsey.

Garters

For the jodhpur-and-paddock-boot crowd only, it is a leather, belt-like "guard" that goes around the child's leg just under the knee. The purpose, besides looks, is to help keep jodhpur legs from riding up, although most jodhpurs have elastic straps under the boot for that purpose.

Formal Attire

Not an evening gown, and not for you, Mom. Some classes, such as a Hunter Classic or a Jumper Classic, either suggest or require formal attire. Unfortunately, these are not the same for each division, so no cross-dressing allowed!

Hunters: Shadbelly (see next page), tan or white breeches, white shirt with stock tie (tying skills needed, unless you choose the pre-tied); plus the rest of the normal gear.

International showjumper Rodrigo Pessoa in formal jumping attire
(photo by Richard Hildreth).

Jumpers: Dark jacket, of the hunter type; white shirt with collar or stock tie, white (the most popular), canary, or fawn breeches, plus the rest of the normal gear: boots, gloves, helmet.

Shadbelly: An unusually fishy name for a riding coat, it's the formal frock coat worn by hunter riders in the Hunter Classic. Black or navy, double-breasted with tails, similar to a dressage shadbelly, but without the shiny brass buttons. More expensive than you want to know. Used is good.

U

The Horse Show Mom: I once called a store named "Outdoor Outfitters" thinking it was the same store that I had seen at a horse show. I inquired about used "Shadbellys" and what sizes they might have in stock. However, the store I had reached was *not* a tack store, and the response was memorable, if not repeatable. Assuming I had reached a teenage clerk, I called again, only to be greeted with more of the same, plus an offer for a variety of fishing gear to go catch my own shad bellies.

SHOWS AND RATINGS

Just as there are rated and non-rated shows, there are rated and non-rated divisions, both of which can occur at a rated show. Rated divisions are those which are recognized by USEF and carry points for National and Zone Year-End Awards. The horse shows themselves are rated based on the number of competitors, the classes offered, and the prize money offered. A letter code is used to identify the rating of these shows and their divisions (Rule XIII).

- A and AA: The highest-rated horse show carrying the most points for year-end national and zone year-end awards. The difference between "A" and "AA" is the prize money offered and the number of points accrued.
- B: Less prize money, fewer classes, fewer points accrued.
- C: Typically a small local show, this show awards the minimum points. However, some divisions at AA shows are rated "C" because they do not carry national points, but do carry points for zone awards.

The non-rated divisions carry no points for USEF, but may often carry points for your state, and occasionally other organizations. This will all become more sensible to you once you've been to a few shows and particularly when you start tracking points.

HUNTERS: THE BIG HEAD SCRATCHER (RULE XXIV)

The hunters are most likely to be your first adventure in a discipline that was, in the author's opinion, designed for the purpose of befuddlement. The very first thing to learn is that your child's horse or pony—not your child—is being judged. The way the horse moves, the way it jumps, and the ease with which the horse responds to your child's direction are all points for the judge to tally. On her side, your child will be required to ride her mount to all the jumps, take the jumps from an appropriate takeoff distance, jump the jumps in order, count and ride the appropriate number of strides to the next jump, finish the course, and make it all look very pretty in the doing. And for all that, the judge is still looking at her horse.

For novice horse show parents, this scenario can be quite frustrating. As proud moms and dads, all we want to see (in the beginning, anyway) is that our child goes around and doesn't fall off. We want to hoot and whistle and clap loudly for our brave youngster and her magically safe mount, and we want her to be rewarded with a bright blue ribbon. In the early days (and sometimes years), we are not savvy about the subtleties of what a "hunter" should look like or how it should move. We haven't yet learned about "chips" and "swapped leads" or "no lead change." You've read the glossary, but really learning what it all means takes time in the field.

The Basics

There are three types of classes of hunters: under saddle, over fences, and model (although model classes are becoming rare). The under saddle class is a flat class judged for the way a hunter horse/pony moves at the walk, trot, and canter in both directions. The ideal horse moves with easy, flowing motion, with very little knee action, ears forward, looking as if he loves his job. Sounds easy, you think? Well, the movement is inherent in the conforma-

tion of the horse. Some horses move like this, but others
knee action at the trot. Some have beautiful movement,
temperaments (the ones with the ears pinned flat back)
looking for the best combination of traits, and it's up to
that she gets her horse to follow the judge's requests fo   ͺ
changes. The most beautiful hunter will not get a ribbon if he refuses to
canter or can't pick up the correct canter lead.

Hunter classes over fences are all basically alike except for the fence
heights. The course typically involves eight fences, two jumped down each
long side of the arena, two jumped on the diagonal going each direction.
The pattern is similar to a figure eight, with the added fences on each long
side. The judge is looking for the same effortless movement, easy temperament, plus a nice rounded form over the jumps. A beautiful horse that hangs
a leg down or hits a rail while jumping will not score as well as one who
picks his knees up evenly over the jump and makes an easy job of the
course.

In a hunter model class, the judge is looking for the ideal conformation. The horse is led in by his handler and asked to stand up squarely in a
line of horses while the judge looks for conformation faults, deformities, or
bumps from injuries. The most beautiful horse wins this class. This class is
always held at big national shows and its purpose is to encourage ideal
breeding.

Hunter classes are grouped into "divisions." Each division involves two
to four classes over fences, and one under saddle class on the flat, also known
as the "hack." Occasionally there will be a "Model" class at non-national
shows.

Divisions of hunter classes are appropriate for different skill levels and
ages, and for amateurs or professionals. These divisions sometimes have unusual names and are defined by their respective jumping height levels. For
example, although there are divisions named "Children's" and "Junior's," this
has to do with fence height, not your child's age. For the professionals
showing inexperienced horses, there are a variety of classes named "Pre-
Green," "1st Year Green," and "Green."

Here are some classes that your child will participate in with her hunter
horse or pony:

Short Stirrup Hunter
(Non-rated)

For your beginning child, usually for ages twelve and under. (Rules vary from state to state, and amazingly, horse show to horse show.) These jumps are 2' to 2'3". It is a basic course built for horses, but can be ridden on ponies. Some shows have a "Long Stirrup Hunter" class of the same height, but for older beginning riders. Generally, once your child has won six blue ribbons in these classes, she becomes ineligible to compete in Short Stirrup. Although different shows have different rules, it's generally felt that if the child is regularly cleaning up in this division, it's time to move up to something more challenging. This benefits both your child and the other children who are still struggling to get some ribbons.

U

The Horse Show Mom: There is nothing quite like this division. The riding is generally terrible, but the mounts are (hopefully) mostly safe. The children are the cutest at this stage; pigtails with huge ribbons, often toothless grins, but the biggest grins nonetheless. The kids have yet to be competition-weary, are still very in love with their horses and ponies, and are at that precious stage of innocence where there is nowhere to go but up.

Beginner/Novice Hunter
(Non-rated)

These classes can be for children or adults, but are sometimes segregated by age. Horse show prize lists will give the qualifications. They are similar to Short Stirrup, with the fence heights going up a small amount to 2'6" to 2'9". The ribbons eligibility rule will also apply here. Once a rider is good enough and has been winning, she should move up.

Children's/Adult Hunter
(C-rated) (Article 2803)

This is a class for children up to age eighteen or adults, with fence heights of 3'. Adults and children may be in and out of the ring before and after

It's always about the ribbons.

each other, but the class is usually pinned separately; the judge is keeping separate "cards" (tally sheets) for the kids and adults. This is an "in-between" division for youngsters who have graduated from the Short Stirrup/Novice or Pony divisions, but haven't mastered the skills for the Junior division's fence heights of 3'6". It is "C" rated by the USEF, which means that it carries points by the USEF for year-end zone awards only. Your child may be year-end champion for her efforts in the Children's division, and get recognition and (hopefully) a tangible memento from your zone. Though there is no national USEF award for the same division, other organizations, such as the Marshall and Sterling League, give year-end awards as long as she is a member. (See Appendix II E, page 237.)

The more important fact about this division is that a good serviceable "Children's/Adult" hunter horse is generally not as expensive as a "Junior" hunter horse. As good horses grow older, their ability to jump higher heights erodes, and it's easier to keep these horses sound over smaller fences.

This is also an aid to the rider, as an older, more experienced horse is so useful for a younger or less experienced rider.

Junior Hunter
(Rated) (Article 2802)

Here is where the competition grows fierce. The fence heights are 3'6", so skill in riding becomes more important, and the quality of the horse becomes all important. At the highest levels, juniors are fighting for a spot at one or all of the "indoor" competitions that happen each fall in various cities on the East Coast. (See Appendix II C, page 227.) The top winners across the nation are invited to compete. At the very highest level, each junior might have two or three horses that they are campaigning, and many of these horses are priced in the serious six-figure range. This information might very well scare you, but take heart; there are other joys in life and other rewarding experiences for your child than going to indoors.

Pony Hunter
(Rated) (Article 2601)

Ah, the Pony division. Perhaps the fiercest competition of all. The fence heights are based on the height of the pony as follows:

- **Small Ponies** (meaning 12.2 hands and under): Fence heights 2'3", riders to be twelve years and younger.
- **Medium Ponies** (over 12.2 to 13.2 hands): Fence heights 2'6", riders fourteen years and younger.
- **Large Ponies** (over 13.2 to 14.2 hands): Fence heights 3', riders eighteen years and younger.

The Pony division is somewhat of a miniature Junior Hunter division. The ponies can be quite handsome and cost fantastic amounts of money. At the top level, competition gets quite intense. The difference is that young children are riding these ponies, and the skill levels are quite varied. Trainers are not allowed to show ponies in the training divisions (a disadvantage over the horse divisions, where a trainer can show a horse earlier in the week to prep it before a young rider's class). In addition, ponies are notoriously smart and can pull a lot of tricks on a kid that can add to inconsistency. The best ponies for this division are older and more experienced, and therefore safer.

U

The Horse Show Mom: Often the parents are the biggest competitors. Standing at the pony ring can be a little reminiscent of the Texas Cheerleading Mom story. Though there is no evidence that one would find a truly murderous parent, one will find several who are willing to hock home and hearth to get their child that fancy mover with the hope that he will put her in the ribbons, and possibly land them a spot at indoor finals. Under pressure from trainers, pressure from their kids, and some kind of weird internal pressure of their own, parents will do some pretty outrageous things to become the parent of a winner. Not at all unlike the author of this book.

Children's Pony Hunter
(Non-rated for national points)
This division is to the Pony Hunter division as the Children's Hunter division is to the Junior Hunters, which translates as lower fence heights and competition that is not as stiff as in the rated Pony Hunter division. The ponies are not as fancy (and therefore not as expensive), making it a good intermediate division between Short Stirrup and the regular Pony division. Or better yet, between ponies and horses.
Note: Some zones carry points for this division toward year-end awards. Check the USEF's Web site for your zone's specific rules.

EQUITATION
(RULE XXII)
These are divisions or classes in which the rider is judged, not the horse. Equitation is an important skill, and most young riders show in both equitation and hunters, very often with the same mount and with good results, until the rider reaches the higher equitation levels, when a horse more suited to and trained for that job usually becomes necessary. A good equitation

rider is well balanced in the saddle and able to give subtle and effective aids to the horse, while giving a smooth and accurate ride.

In a hunter class, the rider typically guides the horse around a simple course on a loose rein. In an equitation class, because the rider asks for more difficult tasks, the horse needs to be both willing and built for the job. He must accept the bit, canter in a nice round frame, and be able to make tight but careful turns. Most riders at the higher levels have a horse that is specifically suited to this job.

An equitation course is similar to that in the hunter ring, but with a few patterns added to test the rider's ability, such as a rollback turn to a jump, a bending line (instead of a straight line between jumps), a narrow jump, a combination, or "in-and-out" (see jump glossary, page 112), or a triple combination (three jumps in a row). Depending on the division or class, the rider may be called back to "test," which means to perform further before the judge. The rider can be asked to perform one or more of nineteen test elements, such as a hand gallop, a counter-canter (on the "wrong lead"), and a halt (see USEF Article 2213). The rider needs to study the course well before the test, so that she remembers the original jump order. Unlike jumper courses, there are no actual numbers on the fences.

The equitation rider is judged on finding good takeoff distances, pace, smoothness, and position in the saddle (Rule XXII, Article 2210). The judge is looking for tight, secure legs, calm and quiet hands, smooth and subtle aids to the horse, and controversially, a certain "look." Although nowhere is it stated that a certain body type is being judged, in a class of similar rounds, the judge will often go for leaner and leggier riders. In a class of dissimilar rounds, the rider who hits the best fence distances will win, no matter how tight the seat or look in the saddle.

Equitation divisions typically consist of two classes: one over fences, one on the flat. They are age specific, with accompanying fence heights. Some typical equitation divisions are:

Short Stirrup Equitation
(Non-rated)
Fence height and age similar to Short Stirrup Hunter: 2' to 2'3", twelve years and under.

Maiden/Novice/Limit Equitation
(Rule XXII, Article 2202)

These fence heights may vary from horse show to horse show, but the range will be from 2' to 2'9", sometimes to 3'. The qualifier will be how many blue ribbons have been won previously, and a restriction may apply that prohibits entering other classes at the show. For example, a rider showing in a rated division of hunters or equitation may not be allowed to enter into a non-rated class or one with lower jumps.

Ribbons won in flat classes, ribbons won in Short Stirrup classes, or any classes with fences lower than 2'3" will not affect the rider's status for these divisions, nor will ribbons won in classes with fewer than six entries.

- **Maiden:** To be eligible to compete in this division, a rider may not have won any blue ribbons other than abovementioned.
- **Novice:** To be eligible to compete in this division, a rider may not have won three blue ribbons.
- **Limit:** To be eligible to compete in this division, a rider may not have won six blue ribbons.

Age-Specific Equitation
(Rule XXII, Article 2211)

Typically the age divisions are as follows:

11 and under: Fences not to exceed 2'6".

12 to 14 years: Fences not to exceed 3'.

15 to 18 years: Fences cannot exceed 3'6" and wings are optional. This allows older children to compete over the higher fences in classes that are not as technically difficult as more advanced "medal" classes.

While these are the upper fence heights limited by USEF rules, many horse shows have lower heights for these divisions.

Riders usually compete all year long and may earn points toward year-end awards for the state (or zones) in which they are held.

Medal Classes

(Rated)

This division, referred to as the "Big Eq," contains the qualifiers for the big national finals, referred to as "indoors" by any savvy parent. There are three major indoor shows at the end of the showing year, during October and November: the Pennsylvania National Horse Show, The National Horse Show, and the Washington International Horse Show. In addition, the USET finals are held on the East Coast in Gladstone, New Jersey, home of the United States Equestrian Team and on the West Coast in varying locations. Each has its own qualification requirements.

The medal classes are single classes over 3'6" fences, some with a second flat phase, and others with a "test" callback for the top four riders (sometimes six) at the end of all the rounds. A typical test might be: "Riders will canter fences 3 and 4, trot fence 8, counter-canter to fence 1, halt after fence 1, canter fence 6, exit the ring at a sitting trot." Judges have the same parameters for testing as in other equitation classes, all found in USEF Rule XXII, Article 2213.

The class is pinned after all four contestants complete the class, the final placement based on a scoring system of 0 to 100. Very good rounds score in the 80s. A score in the low 70s is average. Anything in the 60s means there was an error, such as an add or a chip, and a refusal to jump a fence earns an automatic 40. Information on points and acceptance at finals are found in Appendix II C (page 227).

USEF Medal—3'6"

(Rule XXII, Chapters I and II)

This class is a qualifier for the Medal Finals held at the Pennsylvania National Horse Show in Harrisburg, Pennsylvania, in October. The fence heights are 3'6". The course is technical, with rollback turns, bending lines, and combinations. The top four riders are called back for a test. A rider may move up or down in the top four depending upon how she did in the test, but then the class is pinned to six places. Riders accumulate points throughout the year, and those who accumulate enough points are eligible for the finals, in which usually two hundred or more riders compete. Requirements are found in Appendix II C, pages 227 and 228.

ASPCA Maclay Medal—3'6"

Entrants in this class must be members of the ASPCA, for which application forms are available at most show offices and at www.nhs.org. This championship has been in existence for over fifty years. The classes are judged in two phases: first over fences, then on the flat. The over fences part is similar to a hunter round, although it has its technical challenges. The flat phase is judged on rider position and control.

To win the Maclay finals is the pinnacle of a junior's career, and many of the nation's top professionals were Maclay winners or finalists at the National Horse Show, which until recently was held at Madison Square Garden, and now at the Hudson River's Pier 94 in New York City. Riders accumulate points throughout the year with the point system now identical to the USEF medal, with the exception that qualifiers are invited to a regional final first, with the national invitations being issued to the top riders from each region. Approximately one hundred riders compete at the year-end final.

Washington International Horse Show

This is another national indoor year-end final held in Washington, D.C., or vicinity. Qualifying classes are held at most horse shows and consist of a hunter phase and a jumper phase. A numerical score is given in each, and the combined scores determine the winner. Points are accumulated for the top thirty to thirty-five year-end spots at the finals.

BET/USET

Generously sponsored by Black Entertainment Television, this United States Equestrian Team class seeks to identify future show-jumping stars. The class has a flat phase and then a jumper-style phase over fences that includes a time limit to complete the course. The fences are larger than the other medal classes, with heights to 3'9". Juniors can compete until age twenty-one.

Show Circuit Magazine National Children's Medal-3'

The National Children's Medal was sponsored for many years by Stateline Tack, until 2004, when *Show Circuit* magazine took over this sponsorship. It's a class over 3' fences for juniors who have not yet competed at a 3'6" national final. Points go to a year-end final held in October at the Capital

Challenge Horse Show in Maryland. Typically, those in the top thirty in points won are invited. This is a very good class for juniors just beginning the "Big Eq," and one they can keep doing until they are more confident over the larger fences. It's also very rewarding for juniors who have mounts more suitable to this height.

USEF Pony Medal

In this pony version of the USEF Medal, the jump heights are the same as in the Pony Hunter Division; that is to say, according to pony size. This class allows only one mount per child, and the entire class can either be pinned together—meaning there are no separate height divisions for Small, Medium, and Large Ponies—or pinned separately, depending upon the size of the class. The USEF awards a nice medal when a rider accumulates thirty points, which also qualifies the rider for the annual USEF Pony Finals.

The Marshall and Sterling League

The Marshall and Sterling League is an organization that offers two medal classes as qualifiers for its own year-end final held every fall in Worcester, Massachusetts. Most horse shows offer these classes—the 3' Charles Owen Children's Medal, and the 3'6" HBO Junior Medal.

JUMPERS
(RULE XXVII)

The part of the hunter/jumper discipline that makes sense right from the start are the jumpers, where the cleanest and fastest wins. (The rules are actually a little more complicated, but that's the basic idea.)

Show jumping is an Olympic sport, and in a lesser way is the serious vocation (even as a hobby) of many junior riders. Starting with Pony Jumpers, many kids get the "bug" after having competed in Hunters and Equitation because no faults are given to lack of style on the part of the rider or the horse.

The levels of jumping are based on your child's age, whether her mount is a pony or a horse, and how high the fences are. Sometimes the distances between fences are challenging, other times turns can be daunting. Height is a factor, with the tallest jumps at the Grand Prix level measuring 5' or more.

Scoring

Show jumping scoring is relatively simple. Three things you will have to learn will make the most of your enjoyment as parent and spectator, and for that all important position of educating other parents. They are:

1. **Faults:** These are points given for various mistakes on course.
2. **Levels:** Heights of fences are referred to as levels in the jumper division.
3. **Tables:** The way the class is run. That is, whether it is for optimum time, speed only, or whether or not the class has a jump-off (you'll learn what that is, too) is all covered by a title called a "table."

1. FAULTS
(USEF ARTICLE 2742)

The rule book has a complete description, but the main ones to remember are these:

- Four Faults for knocking down a rail; landing in the water jump (even if it's with only one hoof); knocking down the timing equipment, markers, or flags; the first disobedience on course, known as a refusal; or the horse's stopping or otherwise avoiding a fence (and below Level 5, the second disobedience on course).
- One Fault for each second over the time allowed.
- Elimination: Beyond faults are reasons for elimination, including the fall of a horse or rider, three refusals, going off course, failure to enter the ring within sixty seconds of the start buzzer or starting the course before the judge gives the signal. All of the eliminations are covered in the rule book, Article 2742.

2. LEVELS
(USEF ARTICLE 2719)

Jumping levels are numbered, and those numbers relate to the minimum and maximum height and spread (width) of the fences. The minimums are always 3" below the maximum, and the spreads are as wide as the heights, or 3" more. A quick reference below gives the maximum height:

Level 1: 3'	Level 5: 4'
Level 2: 3'3"	Level 6: 4'3"
Level 3: 3'6"	Level 7: 4'6"
Level 4: 3'9"	Level 8: 4'9"
	Level 9: 5'0"

3. TABLES
(USEF ARTICLES 2743 AND 2744)

Table I: These classes are scored on jumping faults only. There is no "time allowed," and therefore, no need for excessive speed. This is a good class for introducing someone to show jumping, and also a good class to get the kids to "whoa!" down.

Table II: These are clear round classes. That is, those with the lowest scores (penalties) win. Fastest alone does not win. Every clear round remains equal in the placings with other clear rounds.

There are many other subclassifications of jumper tables, and you will hear a lot about IIa, IIb, etc. All can be found in Appendix II D (page 235).

The Money

Jumpers are traditionally a prize money division, which is a great plus if your child wins. However, at the higher levels, the divisions also come with what is known as a "nominating" fee in addition to the class or division fee. This traditionally was only required of the Junior Jumper level and higher, but now many horse shows require it at the Children's level too. The upside is that the payout is bigger. The downside is the classes are huge, and your kid may be competing against adults. Unless she finishes in the top ten or twelve, there's little chance of getting your nominating fee back. The money matters in more than a fiscal way, too; in Junior Jumpers, the horse and rider accumulate points based on the dollar earned: $1=1 point. More on this in the points section in Appendix II B (page 219).

The Divisions

The divisions below are those specifically for junior riders under eighteen years of age, and, although juniors may compete in an Open division, those included here are only the classes for ages eighteen and under.

Pony Jumpers
(Article 2717)

Fence Height 3'6" Maximum

All sizes of ponies may compete in this division, but the height of the jumps is the same, with 3'6" at the highest. Some Small ponies (under 12.2) do a great job in this division, and they're quite a sight to see, but a Large pony with good turning and jumping ability would make the easiest work of the course. There are rules restricting pony riders from competing in certain other Jumper divisions, specifically if the jumps are higher than 3'6".

Children's/Adult Jumpers
(Article 2717)

Fence Height 3'9" Maximum

This combined division for junior and adult riders can sometimes carry quite a lot of prize money, which is split among the top ten riders, whether juniors or adults. Larger venues may have separate classes, according to age, which gives the kids a better chance at the prize money. Riders cannot ride in the Junior Division and the Children's Division at the same show, but they can ride more than one horse. Since this division is rated by each zone, check your zone rules for more information.

Junior/Amateur Owner Division
(Article 2717)

This division typically has two sections: Low and High. The levels are run as separate divisions with their own prize money. The levels are typically as follows: Lows—Level 5 at 4', and Highs—Level 7 at 4'6".

Courses are as tough as the competitors, as the Amateur/Owners are often the best of their bunch, and your kid may have to compete against them in this division.

The prize money is good for those who place well enough to be in the ribbons, although money is sometimes paid to 10th or 12th Place, depending on the horse show. At a large show, the purse can be $10,000 or more for some classics.

THE POINTS

For parents and riders interested in year-end awards and competition finals, this book's section and Appendix II C may be the most read and reread. Calculating points in the different divisions takes a little practice. Keeping track of the points throughout the year requires some attentive record-keeping skills.

A few facts to consider before you start calculating:

- Your child and the horse/pony she is riding must be a member of USEF and USHJA for any points to count. In addition to all other year-end finals, there are also membership requirements. Many of these are covered in Appendix II A (page 217). Your local region or state may have other associations not mentioned, so be sure that you know what you need to belong to in order to be eligible for year-end awards.

- A and AA shows have the highest points. Although it's technically possible to use "B" or "C" show points, the A and AA shows are the best qualifiers for indoors and the Devon Horse Show.

- The USEF's Year-End Horse of the Year Awards are based on points from any rated show, be it A, B, or C. (Again, the USEF's rule book is crucial here for all of the most up-to-date information on the national and zone awards.)

- Classes with more competitors have higher points.

- Ribbon colors indicate points, and it's good to have them memorized:

The Ribbons

1st	Blue Ribbon	10 points
2nd	Red	6 points
3rd	Yellow	4 points
4th	White	2 points
5th	Pink	1 point
6th	Green	½ point
7th	Purple	0 points
8th	Brown	0 points

The ribbons.

Champion and Reserve Champion are 1st and 2nd Places in a division. A division requires more than one class, so these distinctions are not given for single Equitation classes. In the Hunters, Champion and Reserve Champion are awarded bonus points, so most Pony and Junior Hunter moms are skilled at counting these up. The division and horse show ratings carry incremental values for the ribbons points. Point values and calculating tables for these incremental values can be found in Appendix II B (page 219).

ANNUAL FINALS AND YEAR-END AWARDS
USEF Pony Finals

Pony Finals are held every year in August. The qualifying period is July 2 to July 1 every year, and the event moves around, but mostly in the eastern part of the country. This is a wonderful event that hosts roughly 350 or more pony riders every year (by invitation only) in the hunter, equitation, and pony jumper divisions.

In order to be invited, your child must win one championship at any "A" (or "AA") rated show within the qualifying period. Green Ponies may qualify by winning a Champion or Reserve Champion, but only from

December 1 through July 1. The pony may only compete in one of these divisions at Pony Finals. Pony Medal and Pony Jumper finals are held at the same time.

USEF Pony Medal

Invitations to participate in the Pony Medal Final at the USEF's annual Pony Finals are issued to all of those pony riders who have accumulated thirty points during the qualifying year. Points are awarded as follows:

1st Place	= 30 points
2nd Place	= 15 points
3rd Place	= 10 points

USEF Junior Hunter Finals
(USEF Rule XXVIII, Article 2820)

Junior Hunter Finals are also held every year in August, with the same qualifying period as Pony Finals, but held for both the East and West coasts. The venues for these finals move from year to year. Invitations are issued to any Junior Hunter who has won one Champion or Reserve Champion at an "A" (or "AA") rated show during the qualifying period.

Year-End Awards

The USEF awards a Horse of the Year Award (HOTYA) to the top Junior Hunter horses and Hunter Ponies from each of the twelve zones and also to nationwide winners. Awards are given to 6th Place. The Children's Hunters are awarded in each zone, and in some zones, Children's Hunter Ponies are also awarded HOTYA. Zones are delineated by USEF, and the specifications for each zone can be found on the USEF Web site at www.usef.org.

The key issues in keeping points with respect to the USEF Horse of the Year are these:

- National HOTYA points are accrued no matter where the horse show takes place.
- Zone HOTYA points can only be accrued in your home zone, or in USEF-recognized contiguous states. And, for Junior Hunters and

Hunter Ponies, any points calculated for the Zone award are based on a special calculation:

- For A and AA shows, use the B-rated point table
- For C shows, use the C-rated point table
- Some zones host year-end zone finals in the fall, but winning a zone final does not necessarily mean winning the HOTYA. Each zone has its own specifications, and it's best to become familiar with your zone rules.
- Point tabulators are found in Appendix II B (page 220).

HUNTER/JUMPER RESOURCES:
Web Sites

www.bigeq.com: This site has articles and information for junior riders about what's going on nationwide in the equitation ring.

www.chronofhorse: Web site for the weekly magazine, *The Chronicle of the Horse,* which publishes horse show results and news and commentary of interest for those in hunter/jumpers, dressage, and eventing.

www.equisearch.com: Equestrian Web site of Primedia Publications, publisher of *Practical Horseman* and other equestrian magazines.

www.nhs.org: The National Horse Show site with dates and rules for the two National Horse Shows and information about the ASPCA Maclay equitation class and Finals.

www.ryegate.com: Information about the National Children's Medal, results from the larger horse shows, and the Bates Equitation ranking list.

www.usef.org: The United States Equestrian Federation's Web site is a complete resource for rules, show dates, equestrian-related news, and links to many other sites, including the Pennsylvania National Horse Show.

www.wihs.org: The Washington International Horse Show's site, where you can check show information and keep a tally of points.

Books:

Hunter Seat Equitation by George Morris, originally published in 1971, still has much useful information about equitation, and is a good guide for parents and riders interested in understanding the sport.

The Judge is Back by Randy Roy. From the judge's perspective.

Showing for Beginners by Hallie McEvoy. The basics of competition.

Winning: A Training and Showing Guide for Hunter Seat Riders by Anna Jane White-Mullin, is full of photos and training advice.

Scholarship

R. W. Mutch Foundation Equitation Scholarship: Named after well-known judge and illustrator, the late Ronnie Mutch, the R. W. Mutch Foundation offers an annual two-week scholarship to one rider to attend the Winter Equestrian Festival in Florida and train with several top trainers in equitation and jumping. Riders must be riding as fifteen-year-olds and younger during the year that they receive the scholarship. Information is available on the foundation's Web site, www.rwmutch.com.

CHAPTER

10

Dressage

Dressage is a wonderful discipline that takes horses and horsemanship to their most refined level. The movements are gracefully controlled, beautiful, and above all, precise. Of all the equestrian disciplines, the study of dressage is the oldest, going back to early history when horses were trained for the exacting duty of warfare.

Training a dressage horse is like building a complicated piece of machinery, piece by piece. Each sequence must follow the perfection of the previous sequence in training. The end product is a horse that can not only respond to the rider's aids in an amazingly sensitive and seemingly effortless way, but also in a way that makes the horse and rider combination appear so unified and coherent that it is, in a word, breathtaking.

There are hundreds of books written on the subject of dressage and many different approaches to the sport. Dressage enthusiasts are fervent about their sport, almost to the point of religious conviction. As such, there are many dressage interpretations, with fundamentalists and reformists looking at the same arena from different sides of the fence. So many schools of thought, so many ways to express precision, and so many ways to perceive perfection—for this is what dressage is really about: perfection. This is the reason, perhaps, why it has not always been the discipline of choice for small fry. In the United States, basic dressage has been available (in the past) mostly to Pony Club and event riders, and the more successful teenage dressage riders usually got their start in that way.

Young riders across the other disciplines have long remained in the dark about this lovely Olympic-level sport, but that is changing with the introduction of European dressage ponies to the United States. In European countries, dressage is taught early to young riders, even those going on to jumping, as a necessary basic horsemanship skill, useful for both the horse and the rider.

If your child is doing dressage now, you will already be familiar with a few things. You will have watched your child perform at least a low-level dressage test—walking, trotting, and possibly cantering from letter to letter, making circles of 15 to 20 meters, and crossing the arena from one corner to the other, and all the while striving for some inner perfection. For newcomers, some terminology is important to get a grip on what's happening. The glossary here is meant to give a simple overview of common dressage terms. Reference materials cited at the end of the chapter will give interested parents a more in-depth understanding of the sport, along with the more complete glossary at the end of the book.

A BEGINNER'S DRESSAGE GLOSSARY

Alphabet: Well, not the whole alphabet—but you will become very, very familiar with the letters A, B, C, D, E, F, G, H, I, J, K, L, M, P, R, S, V, and X and their unusually illogical arrangement in the dressage arena. A fun mnemonic for remembering the order of the major letters around the arena is this: All King Edward's Horses Canter Many Big Fences. "A" is where the rider enters the arena, and the letters follow along the left side and around in a clockwise manner. (See the diagram on page 155.)

Aids: The signals the rider gives to her horse or pony. Aids include the seat, which is the most important aid; the hands; and the legs. These aids tell the horse when to move forward, move over, back up, walk, trot, canter, and halt—and as you'll learn, a myriad arrangement of other movements. What is never used as an aid in dressage, especially in competition, is the voice. No clucking allowed.

Canter: The horse's natural three-beat gait.

Change of lead: When changing direction at the canter, the horse balances himself by changing the leading leg. This can be done by walking (called a "simple change" of lead), trotting, or at the canter (called a "flying change").

Collection: The horse's body compressed at the gait. Much impulsion and shorter strides.

Counter-Canter: Where the horse canters with the inside front leg leading the outside leg. In some cases, this would be called the "wrong" lead, but the counter-canter is a required movement at the Second Level of dressage and above.

Dressage Queens: Dressage riders with attitude. A derogatory expression, usually aimed at middle-aged amateurs with entitlement issues.

Extension: The horse's body lengthened, with longer strides.

Figures: Required elements such as circles, half-circles, serpentines, and figure eights.

Forehand: The part of the horse in front of the saddle. A horse that is "heavy on the forehand" has his weight shifted to the front and is not using his hind end for the impulsion needed to perform correctly.

Extended.

Freestyle: A type of dressage test, freestyle is a choreographed dressage "dance" with required movements set to music. It is also referred to as "kur" (German for *choice*).

Half-Pass: The horse moves sideways and forward at the same time, its head bent slightly in the direction of the sideways movement.

Impulsion: A favorite and oft-used term describing the desired "motor" the horse can use at the trot and canter. It's never about speed, but about the energy contained in the movements, the "rpms."

Leg yield: Using the leg to push a horse to move to the side while maintaining a forward motion. The horse's legs cross over beneath him. It is a required movement in certain dressage tests.

Level: The division, as in Novice Level or Grand Prix Level.

Passage (sounds like massage): An advanced dressage movement required at Intermediate II and higher, this is one to knock your socks off. This highly suspended trot is beautiful, airy, and dreamlike.

Piaffe: Another movement required at Intermediate II and above, this is a highly collected trot in place or on the spot. Think of the horse dancing in place.

Pirouette: Performed at the canter, this beautiful movement has the horse circling with his forehand while pivoting on one of his hind legs.

Poll: The highest point of the horse's head, right behind the ears.

Renvers: A forward movement where the horse travels with hindquarters bent toward the rail or outside, but the shoulder and head are traveling straight ahead.

Rein-back: Asking the horse to move backwards.

Shadbelly: A formal coat, in navy or black, that is double-breasted with tails.

Stride: One complete horse step at the trot or canter.

Suppleness: Flexibility and smoothness of movement rolled into one tidy expression.

Tempi: Referring to timed changes of lead, called "tempi changes." Advanced level tests require changes of lead to occur every four strides, then two strides, then every stride. Also called "foursies," "twosies," and "onesies." The strides are often referred to as "beats." It's a beautiful thing to watch.

Test: The official movements required of each level. Some levels have four tests, the higher levels each have one very exacting test.

Pirouette.

Throughness: Similar to suppleness, but more specifically the ability of the
   horse to respond throughout his body to the rider's aids.

Travers: An advanced movement where the horse travels forward with
   shoulder to the wall or outside and hindquarters to the inside.

Trot: A two-beat gait. It may be ridden posting or sitting (required at the
   higher levels).

Volte: A small (6-, 8-, or 10-meter) circle.

X: The midpoint of the arena. It is not physically marked; X is the spot for
   the halt and salute to the judge at the beginning of a dressage test.

The United States Dressage Federation (USDF) Directory, an encyclopedia
of dressage information rolled into one compact and portable book, comes
with your USDF membership. Every Horse Show Mom or Dad should carry
it to shows, as it has not only the tests, but a glossary of judging terms, and
a section on dressage protocol. This, in itself, says a lot about the world of

dressage. Here's that word again: precise. You will never be at a loss for information at a dressage show. In a discipline that prides itself on precision, it is not surprising to find lots of help with your everyday horse show protocol.

The USEF rules can be found at the United States Equestrian Federation's Web site at www.usef.org. The rule book explains a lot about dressage, and parents should print it out for themselves and become familiar with it. All of the information here in this chapter is a simplified look at these rules. Where applicable, the USEF rule will be referenced. The Dressage Division is found under Rule XIX.

The United States Dressage Federation also has its own Web site at www.usdf.org. Everything about the dressage organization and competitions (other than the rules) can be found there.

To earn points for year-end awards at USDF-recognized dressage competitions, your child must be a member of the USDF *and* USEF. As of 2004, the membership dues are as follows:

> USDF Junior Membership: $25.00 per year
> USEF Junior Membership: $35.00 per year
> USDF Horse Recording: $65.00 lifetime recording

Being a nicely logical and sequential discipline, dressage can be quite rewarding for your child as she moves up the levels. There are year-end awards, plus cumulative awards for each level that are good goals to focus on, as they not only reward the rider for the work done, but also entice her to continue the training of herself and her horse or pony. But first, she'll need some clothes.

CLOTHING

For the first several years, until your child is ready for Fourth Level, the official dress consists of:

- *Coat:* The rule book states "conservative color," but the norm is black or navy. The dressage coat is short, usually has brass buttons, and is more fitted in style than a hunt coat.
- *Shirt:* White shirts and blouses are usually covered by a stock tie, but riding shirts with chokers are allowed.

Julie Watchover at the collected trot.

- *Stock tie* (for girls, tie for boys): Stock ties are white, and are folded in such a way that they cover the shirt under the coat, and are secured with a pin.
- *Breeches or jodhpurs:* At this level they can be khaki, tan, or white, but white breeches, emulating the pros, seem to be the most popular.
- *Boots:* Brown or black (the norm), tall dress boots or jodhpur/paddock boots.
- *Hat:* Hunt-style hard shell hat, bowler or derby. No top hats or bowlers allowed for Fédération Equestre Internationale pony riders.

Young Riders, Prix St. Georges and Above:
- Dark tailcoat (shadbelly) is worn with a top hat.
- Dark short coat is acceptable also, and is worn with a bowler or hunt cap.
- Breeches: white or light colored.
- Stock tie or man's tie (white).
- Black, tall riding boots.
- Gloves.

ASTM-approved protective helmets are allowed at every level of competition, and no competitor can be penalized for wearing them. Some trainers can be ambivalent about this rule, having gone without for so many years.

Safety should always come first with young riders, and this is your call as a parent. If you feel uncomfortable with your child going unprotected, stand up and tell your trainer.

THE TESTS

Each level has a test that has been written to verify that the training goals of both horse and rider have been met. The tests, which are changed every four years, are available in the USDF Directory or online at www.usdf.org. In addition, laminated booklets which also include diagrams of the arena (and are called "Whinny Widgets") are available at most tack stores, and online at both USEF and USDF. This is where those arena letters come into use.

An example of the movements required at an Introductory level test would be :

1. **A**   Enter at working trot.
   X   Halt. Salute. Proceed at working trot.
2. **C**   Track right.
   B   Turn right.
3. **X**   Circle right 20 meters diameter working trot.
             On returning to X
4. **X**   Circle left 20 meters diameter.
             On returning to X
   XE   Working trot.
5. **E**   Track left.
   Between A&F   Working canter left.
6. **F**   Working canter around the arena to E.
   E   Working trot.
7. **K**   Working walk.
   A   Halt. Immobility four seconds.
             Proceed at medium walk.
8. **FXH**   Change rein at free walk on a loose rein.
   H   Working walk.
9. **Between H&C**   Working trot.
   Between C&M   Working canter.
10. **M**   Working canter around the arena to H.

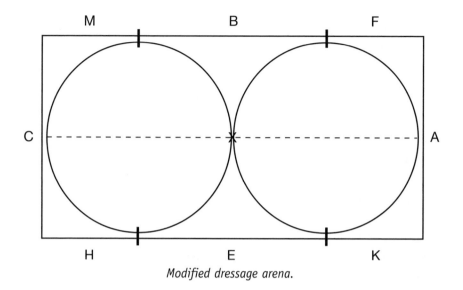

Modified dressage arena.

11. **H**   Working trot.
    M   Working walk.
12. **B**   Half-circle right, 10 meter diameter to X.
    X   Half-circle left, 10 meter diameter to E.
13. **K**   Working trot.
    A   Down center line.
    X   Halt, salute.
            Leave arena on a long rein at A.

The movements in any dressage test are repeated going both ways (right and left) so that the judge can see if the horse is balanced (and not "one-sided") to both sides. As your child progresses, she will move up through the levels to more difficult movements and performance.

JUDGING

After competing, each rider gets a test booklet with scores and comments from the judge(s) on each and every required move made during the test. This is the ultimate in equestrian judging. No other discipline (other than the dressage of eventing), provides so much feedback for the rider. It is a wonderful (if double-edged) sword. Feedback, whether positive or negative, gives the rider the tools to build to the next level. On the other hand, not everyone wants such a detailed overview of what perhaps was a less than stellar performance, and there are always those little differences of opinion that happen whenever a subjective sport gets judged. Dressage, for all of its prescribed moves and precise definitions, is still subjective. Some judges will like the way your child performed her canter depart; others will find fault with the horse's millisecond unwillingness. Nonetheless, in the big scheme of all equestrian sports, the way a dressage class gets judged is a wonderful gift to the rider.

A scribe sitting beside the judge writes down the scores and comments, so the judge can keep her attention on the ring. The scale is 1 to 10, with 10 being excellent and 0 for not performed. The scores for each movement are added together and divided by the total number of points possible to give a percentage score. The better the percentage, the better the overall score. Scores in the 60+ percentile are considered very good.

Certain parts of the test have what is called a "coefficient"—a multiplier of two—so those marks with a coefficient are doubled. At the end of the test there are "collective" marks that give general points: gaits, impulsion, submission, and the rider's position. These also have a coefficient of two, and those points will be added to the total. The total score received is divided by the total possible, giving a percentage score.

THE LEVELS

Progress in dressage is tested through the levels. Each level, starting with Introductory, has specific goals and a specific competitive test. The following is a brief explanation of the purpose of each level and the test movements required.

Introductory Level

The most basic level has two tests, A and B. They require a walk and posting trot but no canter, and demonstrate the most basic skills of the horse and rider. That does not mean that there is no skill required. Straightness begins here as the foundation for all of the upper levels. This is the beginning of a long training relationship that gets better and better if each step follows the previous. In other words, no jumping ahead!

Training Level

For training level, there are four tests. Each one is progressively more difficult than the previous. The purpose is to reinforce the notion that the horse accepts the bit, moves forward willingly, and is supple and light in his movement. Movements include walk, trot, canter, circles, half-circles, loops, and a large circle while allowing the horse to stretch down and forward at the trot.

First Level

Moving up to First Level requires more skill for both the horse and rider. This level has four tests and requires change of lead through the trot, leg yields, and the beginning of attention to extension and collection. The purpose is to show throughness and thrust, the beginning of impulsion.

Second Level

Building on the previous work—shoulder in, travers, renvers, a simple change of lead, rein-back, and a turn on the haunches are all introduced at this level. More suppleness, straightness, and progression of collection that requires the horse to carry more and more weight on his hindquarters are the goals at this level.

Third Level

Greater ability to show the transitions from collected to extended gaits, half-pass at a trot, and single flying lead change are introduced at this level. The goal is to demonstrate smooth and obvious transitions from extended and collected movements.

Fourth Level

The movements at this level should be supple, smooth, and reliable. The transitions must be very clear and precise. Quarter pirouettes and tempi changes (every fourth stride) are introduced in the three tests offered here.

FEI Levels

The Fédération Equestre Internationale is the worldwide organization that monitors competitions at the highest international levels. They make the test requirements at this level so that competitors in all countries are competing with the same skill and ability, such as at the NAYRC (North American Young Riders Championship). For junior and young riders, the following are FEI equivalents:

> FEI Pony Tests: Second Level
> FEI Junior Team and Individual Tests: Fourth Level, test 1
> FEI Young Rider tests: Prix St. Georges

The following levels of dressage are *all* FEI levels. Though it may be some time before your child competes at this level, here is an overview:

PRIX ST-GEORGES

Although this is described in the USEF rule book as a test of "medium" standard, Prix St. Georges level requires a lot of skill for both horse and rider. The horse is now ready to perform all of the previously tested moves in combination and with great skill and accuracy, and the rider must show that she can execute the test without overt and obvious aids. The test includes eight-meter voltes, three- and four-stride tempi changes to both directions, counter-canters, half-pirouettes, and more.

INTERMEDIATE I

Again, a name that sounds like a simple test, but not exactly what it appears. At this level, the goal is Grand Prix, for which this is a stepping-stone. Now we see two- and three-stride tempi changes, pirouettes, and complicated half-passes with flying changes.

INTERMEDIATE II

One stop below the pinnacle of Grand Prix, this test shows off the rider's professional-quality equitation abilities. The horse is a highly tuned and perfected, precise machine. Passage, piaffe, and one-stride tempi changes are just a few of the wonderful movements at this level.

GRAND PRIX
Divided into two separate tests, Grand Prix B and Grand Prix Special, these tests include all of the classical movements, and impulsion is the queen of the day. Grand Prix Special is the same as A and B, but the transitions are more important in the judging of the class.

Freestyle
Freestyle (also called "Kur") is in a league all its own, and is very exciting to watch. Riders can begin doing freestyle at First Level. The movements must strictly adhere to the level being shown, and advanced movements are forbidden. The rider is free to pick suitable music and design the test to her liking (the judges are given a copy beforehand). There are compulsory movements for each level, which can be found in the USDF Dressage Directory and in the USEF's rule book at www.usef.org.

THE COMPETITIONS
Now that you have a preliminary understanding of the levels, you are ready to accompany your child to a horse show. Dressage shows are very tidy and prescribed affairs. Everyone is on time (or at least expected to be), and everyone seems to know what is expected. There is no concierge to explain the way to your ring or the snack bar, but if you act like you know what you're doing, you'll be right at home with the rest of us who are similarly befuddled, but cool in our demeanor.

Schooling shows are a great start, as you have more relaxed competitors. Since no one is counting on earning points for any year-end awards, they can afford to be unperturbed by the stress of competition. Everyone also tends to have more fun at these venues—but it does not mean that some people won't take the competition very seriously. That is the nature of a discipline that requires focused attention and appeals to large numbers of exceedingly goal-oriented middle-aged women (not unlike this author).

Recognized shows can be different from venue to venue. Your trainer is likely to know which shows are more competitive, and which shows will allow your child some success without having to compete against large numbers. Dressage is not yet filled with large numbers of young kids like the other equestrian disciplines, even at the pony level.

The divisions at the shows are usually Open, Adult Amateur, and Junior/Young Rider (twenty-one and under). The USEF lists the following age classifications, but most shows do not have separate divisions for these FEI divisions:

Children: Ages 12 to 14
Pony Riders: Ages 12 to 16
Juniors: Ages 14 to 18
Young Riders: Ages 16 to 21

As you can see, there is a little overlapping of the age distinctions.

In Europe, it is typical for kids to compete on ponies until they are sixteen years old. In the U.S., anyone can ride a pony at a USEF show, but in a class or division specifically for ponies, the limit is age sixteen.

Young Riders is a special program for up-and-coming talent, and as such, across the disciplines, all "Young Riders" compete until they are twenty-one years old.

Your child's age, according to USDF and USEF rules, is what she happens to be on the first day of the USEF calendar year, which in this case starts on December 1. So, if your child's birthday is December 2, and for example, in 2005 she turns fifteen, for all of 2006 she will compete as a fourteen-year-old. This is to her great advantage if she is competing as a Young Rider. It essentially gives her a whole extra year to compete at that level before she has to move on to the Adult Amateur level.

In addition to your child being ready and dressed, her horse must also be braided and groomed to win. Braids may be done in rubber bands, yarn, white tape, or whatever the currently popular style dictates. Braiding can be done the night before if you can be sure that the horse won't rub them out in his stall. Clean shiny coats (for both horse and rider) are a must, but the fancy little white boots that are used for schooling and making the horses and ponies look so cute are actually forbidden in the ring. Dressage whips must be a certain length (43" maximum) and different levels require different bridles and bits. Lots of rules, lots of things to think about, and lots of Mom's help. That's what horse showing is all about.

BIG SHOWS

Once your child is doing well, she will inevitably catch the bug to go for more honors and awards. Dressage, being the orderly and progressive discipline that it is, has many stars for your young one to shoot for. Some are individual championships, some are stepping-stone achievements, and others are team competitions. As you become more familiar with the sport, you will come to know these well. Here are a few highlights:

Regional Championships

For the nine USDF national regions, the Great American Insurance Group sponsors the USDF Championships every year. Riders qualify as a horse/rider combination to participate by competing in special USDF Championship classes at participating horse shows. Training Level through Intermediate I are offered for Junior/Young Riders, and the more advanced classes are offered in the Open division. All riders and horses must be members of both the USDF and USEF, and horses must be life recorded with the USDF. Qualifying to compete at the Regional Championships requires paying $10.00 (the qualifying ride fee for each test), and earning specific scores in at least two tests. The scores must also be earned in the highest level of the test. For example: First Level—Test 4, or Third Level—Test 3. The rules may change from year to year, so it's best to check on the USDF's Web site: www.usdf.org.

Champion and Reserve Champion at the finals are awarded prize money, either as cash or scholarship. Every rider who qualified is mailed a commemorative certificate, and all those who participate are awarded special pins.

Dressage Seat Medal Finals

Dressage equitation, a relatively new aspect of the sport, encourages and rewards good position and correct use of the aids, and as such, judges the rider rather than the horse. The Dressage Seat Medal Finals, inaugurated in

2003, are held every year in conjunction with a Regional Junior/Young Rider Championships. Any rider qualified for a Regional Championship may participate in the Dressage Seat Medal semi-finals held at each Regional Championship. The top two from each age division are invited to the Medal Finals. The riders may ride borrowed horses, allowing those who come from long distances to participate.

Detailed information on how the classes are judged can be found at www.usef.org under the Equestrian Sports section.

NAYRC

The North American Young Riders Championship is a special event for youngsters aged sixteen to twenty-one who ride at the Fourth Level and above. It is an event held every August, often in the Chicago area, and includes the other Olympic disciplines of eventing and show jumping. This

Samantha Booth, Rocky Mountain Dressage Society's 2003 First Level Junior Champion.

sponsored program allows young American riders to compete against the best from United States, Canada, Mexico, Bermuda, and the Caribbean Islands. Top riders from each region are sent for both a team and an individual competition. More information can be obtained at www.usef.org.

USEF FEI Junior Championships

Much like the NAYRC, the Junior Championships are an FEI-approved competition for riders ages fourteen to eighteen who have not competed above Prix St. Georges Level. Riders may compete in both the Junior Championship and the NAYRC, but not in the same year. Riders are qualified as horse/rider combinations and must meet the following criteria:

1. Five scores from five different judges from three FEI Junior Team Tests and two FEI Junior Individual Tests.
2. Scores must be an average of 60 percent or higher.
3. The submission date is around mid-June (check with the USDF for current dates).
4. All scores must be submitted in order to be considered for the team. Applications are available on the USDF Web site or by contacting the USEF's Dressage Department.

The top twelve riders, with two alternates, will be invited to compete. Three teams of four members each compete as both individuals and teams, riding the FEI Junior Team and Individual dressage tests.

USDF Regional Youth Team Championships

For all riders under twenty-one, this is a great event held annually in each region. From Introductory Level to Grand Prix, riders can compete as part of a team. There is no qualification necessary to participate, and riders enjoy an event that includes clinics with top trainers and get-togethers with other competitors.

USDF AWARDS

The USDF has a wonderfully organized program for recognizing achievement at all the levels. Riders and their horses can earn awards over the course of their careers. The results from each horse show go toward these awards, provided that qualifying scores are 60 percent or higher and have been earned at a USDF/USEF-recognized competition.

Rider Performance Award: This applies to Training, First, and Second levels and is based on scores from at least two competitions, four judges, and four different classes. Your child could attend two shows in the whole year and receive this award as long as she got the 60 percent in two classes per show, and was judged by different judges in each class. A patch and certificate are awarded.

Bronze Medal Rider Award: Six scores are required, two each at First, Second, and Third levels from two different judges and rides at each level. A medal and certificate are presented for this award (now you know why some kids have medals on their jackets).

Silver Medal Rider Award: This is based on four scores (two from Fourth Level, and two at Prix St. Georges), with each being from two judges and two different rides. A medal and a certificate are presented.

Gold Medal Rider Award: This is based on four scores (two from Intermediate I or II, and two from Grand Prix), with each being from two judges and two rides. Go for the Gold.

USDF Musical Freestyle Rider Award: A bronze, silver, or gold medal must be won before a Freestyle Bar can be won at that particular level, but a rider can earn both a medal and a freestyle bar in one year.

Freestyle Bronze Award: This requires scores of 65 percent and higher with two freestyle scores at First level, two at Second Level, two at Third Level, and each with two judges and two rides.

Freestyle Silver Bar Award: Again, 65 percent or higher, four scores at Fourth Level, with four judges and four rides.

Freestyle Gold Bar Award: Scores of 65 percent and higher, with two freestyle Intermediate I and two at Grand Prix, with two separate rides and two different judges for each level.

In addition to the medals and bars for riders, there are awards for horse/rider combinations. In this case, horse and rider are a team, and as such, must remain so to qualify for a particular level.

The Junior/Young Rider Awards

- Training, First, Second, Third, and Fourth Levels. A minimum of eight scores from four different judges and four different competitions. The scores need to be a median of 60 percent or higher, and two of those scores need to be 58 percent or higher from the highest test in that particular level.

- Prix St. Georges, Intermediate I, Intermediate II, and Grand Prix. Median scores of 58 percent or higher from four different judges and four different competitions.

Note: Figuring median scores takes a little math and some understanding of the rules. Your USDF Directory is the source for this information (and a lot of other good info, too).

DRESSAGE RESOURCES

www.chronofhorse.com: Web site for the weekly magazine, *The Chronicle of the Horse,* which publishes horse show results and news and commentary of interest for those in hunter/jumpers, dressage, and eventing.

www.equisearch.com: Primedia, Inc. Web site with articles, news, and links for all horse disciplines.

www.usdf.org: The official Web site of the the United States Dressage Federation offers information about shows, national competitions, and upcoming area events. The organization also publishes *USDF Connection,* a magazine for its members.

www.usef.org: The United States Equestrian Federation's Web site has the official dressage rules, tests, show dates, and more.

Publications

Dressage Today: An informative magazine published by Primedia, Inc.

USDF Connection: Official magazine of USDF.

Whinny Widgets: Instructor's Dressage Test Book, by Kitti DeWitt, is a wonderful laminated, spiral-bound book with all the tests and explanations of the goals of the movements. The Web site (www.whinnywidgets.com) also offers test booklet holders and small spiral-bound individual tests.

Eventing

Rolling countryside, ditches, brooks, billowy clouds against stark blue skies, air as crisp as new linen: these are the backdrops for eventing, sometimes known as combined training. Although the discipline includes dressage and show jumping, nothing brings the sport to mind more precisely than the vision of galloping Thoroughbreds, breathtaking (and breath-stopping) jumps, and mile-wide grins of competitors as they cross the finish line of their cross-country course. Half sister to fox hunting, brother to steeple-chasing, cousin of endurance, and virtual parent of Pony Club, eventing combines so much under one roof, albeit the open-domed roof of sky.

Olympic gold medalists have inspired thousands of youngsters to brave the ditches, soar over obstacles, and needle their parents until they too are willing partners and participants. And whether, as parents, you participate as a jump judge, groom, boot polisher, tailor, trailer hauler, or merely financier, this sport is one to draw you in, wrap its arms around you, and turn you back out as a parent who can love the outdoors no matter the weather, and who can breathe (eventually) as your child and horse make it down that bank, across the ditch, and back up the hill. You'll also learn to appreciate the more subtle aspects of horsemanship, such as dressage and the amazing endurance ability of eventing horses.

Eventing's other name—"combined training"—explains the thoroughness of this sport. The same horse and rider combination aspire to excel in the focused and refined discipline of dressage, then set off to the

Eventing—Yeehah!

cross-country portion to prove their brave boldness, and finally go back to the jumping ring where they still need energetic attention to clear a round of stadium jumps.

You may have come to this discipline by accident. That is, it may have been the only one available when your little one begged to learn to ride. You may be an experienced foxhunter, or your child may have started in Pony Club, but for whatever reason, you're there, you love it (or will), and you learn and benefit as your child continues on in her career.

Many eventers started as Pony Clubbers, and the United States Pony Club (USPC) can list many Olympians as its graduates. Pony Club compe-

Coming back from the cross-country course.

titions are similar to eventing competitions, and many children have their first competitive experience at a Pony Club rally. The USPC has its own rules, and many books have been written about the Pony Club, both the U.S. Club and its founder, the British Pony Club. This chapter will not cover USPC rules, but at the end of the chapter you will find information about their books and contacts.

A lot of changes have taken place in the last few years in eventing. The official organization has even undergone a name change, from United States Combined Training Association (USCTA) to United States Eventing Association (USEA). Some of the changes are happening due to the large venues required to hold competitions (hampered by the shrinking amount of available real estate), plus the huge financial and time commitments required to staff a three-day event, the pinnacle of eventing competitions. But this is also a sport where Americans excel in international competition; witness the silver and bronze medals at the most recent Olympics, and the ensuing inspiration to youngsters that will help to ensure its continued popularity amongst equestrians.

A BEGINNER'S EVENTING GLOSSARY

Here are a few essential eventing terms:

Collected: Used in dressage, this movement at the trot or canter results in the horse's stride being shorter and the "frame" of the horse being more compact.

Combination: Certain obstacles that are doubled or tripled in a line. They are jumped individually, but the jump is considered a single obstacle with two or more parts or elements. Such obstacles will be marked, for example, "13 a, b, and c."

Cross-Country: The speed and endurance part of eventing. Cross-country is just that: riding across open country at a gallop and jumping natural and man-made obstacles such as water elements, streams, or small pools. At Events (either two-day or three-day), historically, cross-country has been just one element of the speed and endurance test. The other phases are:

- *Roads and Tracks:* The horse and rider cover this course within an allotted time, at a trot or slow canter. The course has no jumps. Roads and Tracks are phases A and C of the cross-country test at events.
- *Steeplechase:* Historically deriving its name from an informal race across country toward a church steeple, the Steeplechase (in itself its own racing discipline) is a timed event over brush obstacles, caried out at a gallop. It is phase B of the test.
- *Cross-Country:* Phase D of the test.

Note: At the time of this writing, much talk was going on about the future of the roads and tracks and the steeplechase phases. Sections A, B, and C were officially removed from the 2004 Olympic competition.

Dressage: Dressage is a specific method of training a horse to respond to the rider's aids in such a way that the horse develops its muscles and movements to its best advantage. Used for centuries in military training, it is considered the "classical" way to train a horse. In competitive dressage, horse and rider are required to perform specific "tests" (here's that term again) consisting of prescribed movements, to be done accurately and in sequence. Each level has its own test, with the higher-level movements becoming progressively more difficult, but always building specifically on each foundation movement of the previous level. Dressage is an Olympic competitive discipline within its own right; the dressage test at an eventing competition is different from one at a dressage competition. See more dressage terms on pages 148–151 in the Dressage chapter.

Event: The official name of an eventing competition. Specifically refers to two- and three-day events, but may be used casually in reference to mini-events (an unrecognized schooling type competition), tests, horse trials, or Pony Club rallies.

Fences: see Obstacles.

Horse trial: A type of event, qualifying one to participate at three-day events. It is also another term for an event. See page 178.

Obstacle: This is the general term given to arena jumps and cross-country jumps. The arena jumps are covered in Chapter 9 (page 114). In cross-country, obstacles are marked by red and white flags, with the

Heading for the obstacle.

red flag on the right side of the jump and the white flag on the left. Yellow directional markers help the competitors stay on course. Each obstacle has a sequential number, and at each level of competition the numbers are color coded as such:

- Advanced: White on a blue background
- Intermediate: White on a red background
- Preliminary: White on a green background
- Training: White on a black background
- Novice: Black on a white background

This distinction helps to prevent a novice rider from trying to scale an advanced obstacle by mistake. Obstacles include the following:

- *Bank:* Not the building where you withdraw all that horse show money! A bank (or embankment) is a steep decline or incline in the land, often with another element at the bottom, such as water, a ditch, or a fence.
- *Bullfinch:* A fence that has high brush coming out of the top. The brush is thin, and can be jumped through.
- *Coffin:* An unseemly name for an obstacle, it consists of a ditch between two fences, with the ground sloping down between the fences toward the ditch.
- *Coop:* A triangular box jump that is supposed to resemble a chicken coop.
- *Ditch:* A depression in the ground that needs to be crossed. Sometimes a ditch is on the other side of a jump, or it can be between two jumps, where the horse lands from the first jump, jumps the ditch, and immediately jumps another fence.
- *Drop:* An obstacle that has a landing side lower than the takeoff side. The measurement of the drop is from the top of the fence to the lowest point of the landing side.
- *Element:* A component of an obstacle.
- *Keyhole:* Usually made with brush, this obstacle is a hole that the horse and rider jump through (usually seen at the higher levels).
- *Water elements:* A brook or small pool of water. In show jumping, an artificial pool of water with a rail over it is known as a Liverpool.

- *Oxer:* This is basically two jumps close together, to be jumped as one. The higher the jumps, the wider the spread.
- *Trakehner:* A fence set into a ditch.

Show Jumping: This is the third required element of a horse trial or event. Held in an arena, it is a timed event with several jumps to be jumped, with at least one change of direction. The obstacle heights are determined according to the rules for the level of competition. There is an optimum time allowed, but the rounds are not scored on speed. The object is to jump the obstacles within the optimum time, in the correct order, and without knocking down any of the rails. A complete list of fences can be found on page 114 in the hunter/jumper chapter.

Spread: This is the distance across a jump or obstacle. Spreads are measured from the highest point of a jump—the base—or across an obstacle without height, such as water. Each level of competition has parameters for spread lengths.

Test: This term, used for many different things, can be a little confusing:

- A dressage "test" (as noted above): The necessary movements prescribed for a dressage phase of a horse trial or an event.
- Test: A competition, one below the level of a horse trial.
- Combined test: A competition requiring two of the three phases of eventing.
- Individual test: A competition requiring only one of the three phases of eventing.

MEMBERSHIPS

Once your child is ready for a recognized competition, if she is competing at Novice level or higher, she and her horse or pony must first be registered with the USEA (United States Eventing Association). Once she begins competing at the Preliminary Level or above, she will also need to become a member of the United States Equestrian Federation (or pay a non-member fee each time she competes). She will register as a Junior member until she is eighteen, and a Young Rider member until she is age twenty-one.

Age Qualifications

Every equestrian organization has its own version of the calendar. The USEA considers your child's age based on the calendar year in which she reaches a qualifying age. That means, from January 1 of the year your child reaches eighteen, she is considered an eighteen-year-old. The USEF, on the other hand, considers December 1 to be the beginning of their year, and if your daughter is age seventeen on December 1, she remains so in the eyes of the USEF until December 1 of the next year. This should not make a difference to you if she restricts her competing to eventing. If she occasionally participates in a rated hunter/jumper show, you'll have to remind yourself of her "official" showing age. There is a distinction between "Junior" and "Young Rider." Junior applies to all youth eighteen and under; Young Rider refers to those ages nineteen to twenty-one.

Membership applications are available online from both organizations. As of 2005, the fees were:

USEA: $50 for Junior Members (18 and under)

$75 for Young Riders or Full Members (19 and over)

$25 one-time fee for any non-member competing in Beginner Novice Level in lieu of a yearly membership. This would only make sense if your child were to do one event per year.

Horse Life Recording: $125. A limited recording can be obtained for $25 for horses competing in Novice and Training levels only. Once the horse moves up, the $25 can be applied to a full recording.

USEF: $45 per year buys a Junior membership until your child is 18 on December 1. (Not necessary at Training Level and below.)

CLOTHING (ARTICLE 1713)

Like most disciplines, there are "rules" about show dress, and then there are trends. Every year someone has a new take on an old favorite, and you can drive yourself nuts trying to keep up. Your child will grow quickly enough through her mid-teen years for you to always have an option to buy something new.

The clothes outlined below are based on the rule book requirements, and divided into what you need for each phase. Fortunately, there will be some overlapping.

Cross-country

Breeches or jodhpurs: Any color.

Shirt: Polo shirt (any color).

Vest: Approved safety vest.

Head gear: ASTM-approved helmet with chin harness, usually with a colorful cap cover.

Boots: Field, dress, or jodhpur/paddock boots in black or brown. Field boots are tall boots with laces in the front at the ankle; dress boots are tall without laces; jodhpur or laced paddock boots are short and worn only with jodhpur-style breeches.

Gloves: Optional.

Ally Berman in cross-country attire (photo by Harriet Berman).

Dressage

Breeches: Light tan, khaki, or white.

Head gear: Hunt-style cap in black or dark blue. After Intermediate level, a
   top hat is allowed.

Shirt: White or light-colored dress shirt with stock tie and pin (or choker
   for girls, tie for boys).

Jacket: Novice through Preliminary: Dark color or tweed.

Intermediate and Advanced: No tweed allowed. If shadbelly is worn, a top
   hat is required.

Boots: Same as for cross-country, except black dress boots are preferred at
   Intermediate and Advanced levels.

Gloves: Novice through Preliminary: optional dark color, tan, beige, or white.
   Intermediate and Advanced: Mandatory white or dark color.

Show Jumping

Head gear: ASTM-approved protective head gear with chin harness, black
   or dark blue solid.

Dressage test ready (photo by Harriet Berman).

Jacket: Novice though Preliminary: dark or tweed hunt coat. Intermediate through Advanced: no tweed allowed.

Boots: Same as for cross-country.

Breeches: Light color or white.

Shirt: Dress shirt with stock and pin; choker or tie.

Gloves: Optional: dark color, tan, beige, white.

THE COMPETITIONS

Each type of competition has its own United States Equestrian Federation (USEF) rules, and any rule covered here is referred to

Young Rider Brittany Kart ready for her stadium jumping round.

at the end of each definition. The rules are available online at www. useventing.com, and also at www.equestrian.org. What is offered here is merely an overview. Print out a copy of the official rules and keep it for reference. As you become familiar with all of the nuances of eventing, the rules will make more sense; plus you can impress the other parents with your knowledge!

The following are the official names of recognized eventing competitions: Test, Horse Trial, Three-Day Event (which, as you will see below, can last up to five days).

Test

Normally taking place on one day, a test can be either individual or combined; that is, one of the phases for individual, or any two for combined: dressage and show jumping, dressage and cross-country, or show jumping and cross-country—or all three can be offered in one day. A test is a good introduction to the world of eventing, and a great starting place for your child's show career. There are several classifications of these tests (USEF Article 1721):

- **Cross-Country Test:** The use of various cross-country skills are tested (USEF Article 1723).
- **Combined Test:** Any two combinations of the three phases: dressage, cross-country, and jumping, or two different cross-country tests. The same horse must be used for both tests (USEF Article 1724).
- **Starter Event Rider Test:** For riders new to competition (specifically, having never competed in a Horse Trial), this has elements of all three phases, but shortened, with fences 2'6" or under. Riders can be any age, and use any horse (USEF Article 1725).
- **Eventing Equitation Test:** Similar in structure to a Combined Test, riders ages fourteen to eighteen participate in a short dressage test and jump ten or so cross-country type jumps, but the jumps may be in an arena *or* a field. Jumps are bigger than the Starter Event test, 3'7" and under. The rider is judged on seat, position, and the effectiveness of her aids. The same horse must be used for both tests (USEF Article 1726).
- **Young Event Horse Trials:** Any rider can ride this, but the *horse* must be four or five years old and never have competed at a regular Horse Trial at the Preliminary Level. Includes dressage, show jumping, and in-hand for conformation. A good rule of thumb to remember here is this: A younger horse always requires a more skilled rider. Young Event horse trials are usually ridden by professionals.

Horse Trial

A competition where there are three tests—dressage, cross-country, and show jumping—normally held over two or three days; but just to keep you on your toes, it can be held in one day. The dressage test is always first, followed by the other two in any order. Eligibility rules govern who can participate in horse trials, and certain levels of horse trials are qualifiers to compete in a two-day or three-day event. International horse trials run under FEI rules are called CICs, and are given one, two, or three stars. See the next page for an explanation of the starring system.

Two-Day or Three-Day Events

TWO DAY

An event held over two days, including all three tests in this order (USEF Article 1751):

1. Dressage
2. Show Jumping
3. Cross-Country, but in four phases:
   Phases A and C: Roads and Tracks
   Phase B: Steeplechase
   Phase D: Cross-Country Obstacles

THREE-DAY

Three distinct tests, each held on separate days, but the number of competitors may require the actual event to be held over four or five days to accommodate all the dressage tests. They take place in the following order:

1. Dressage
2. Cross-Country (in the same four phases as above)
3. Show Jumping

In addition, each three-day event is rated and starred according to its level and participation by foreign countries. The categories are as follows:

1. International Three-Day Event (CCI)
2. Official International Three-Day Event (CCIO), an official team competition
3. International Championship Three-Day Event (CH)

If you are new to this sport, you won't need to become familiar with these upper-level competitions for your child's sake just yet, but bragging rights do apply if you can rattle off these initials with bold assurance.

The levels of three-day events are as follows:

1. *One Star* (★): One-star events serve as an introduction to the three-day events for riders and horses.
2. *Two Star* (★★): These are for competitors just beginning international competition.
3. *Three Star* (★★★): For those rising stars with international experience
4. *Four Star* (★★★★): For the top tier in the sport, both riders and horses.

So, just for a recap, the recognized competitions are as such, in ascending order of difficulty and "rating": Test, Horse Trial (including CIC), Two-Day

Event, ★Three-Day Event, ★★Three-Day Event, ★★★Three-Day Event, ★★★★Three-Day Event.

Each division has a name and is related to the height of the jumps and relative difficulty of the course and test. Your child will obviously start in the lower levels and move up as she is ready, a very important point for you to consider. Eventing is a wonderful and exciting sport, but any equestrian sport has inherent dangers if care is not taken for the readiness of the rider and the horse. The best trainers would not think of "over-facing" a child or her horse to jumps and courses too advanced for her abilities. Doing so is a well-worn recipe for disaster. As parents, *we* have to watch for two things:

1. *Safety:* When we see our child and her horse ride and jump, she should look safe and in control of her mount. Trust in your trainer is important, but trust in your own parental intuition is primary.

2. *Confidence:* This can be a double-edged sword. An overconfident child can be reckless, taking risks that are dangerous. An underconfident child can allow her anxiety to penetrate to her horse, making the horse nervous and indecisive at the jumps, leading to accidents. The right amount of confidence is when the child has a safe, reliable horse that she can have good reason to trust, and she trusts her own ability to navigate the course before her. This comes with good training, practice, experience, and riding a course that is appropriate to the ability of both rider and mount.

U

The Horse Show Mom: As parents we might consider unthinkable the notion that any trainer would allow a child to be in an unsafe situation with a horse; to give the human species credit, carelessness is not a goal for most trainers. But some horsepeople are their own species of hardworking, fearless, pain-enduring, adrenaline-addicted cowboys, no matter the gender or equestrian discipline. We have all heard variations of the trainer who admonishes an injured child to get back in the saddle, who yells at a kid with a broken arm for crying, and who demands their own standard of toughness and pain tolerance with their students. Parents are sometimes intimidated by their kids' trainers to the point of inaction. We can also be intimidated by our own competitive drive to see our kids be tough and succeed. Horses and kids are a wonderfully exhilarating combination, but a dangerous one nonetheless. Never be afraid to step in if you have a feeling that your child is in an unsafe situation, that her pain may be more than what it appears, or that a stiff upper lip is actually concealing a broken bone.

THE LEVELS
(USEF APPENDIX 1)

The levels are defined by parameters of difficulty for each phase. The dressage tests are defined and revised every few years for each level, and are consistent throughout each horse trial or event. Show jumping levels are defined by height, number of jumps, and the allowed time. Cross-country levels are defined by the length of the course (in meters), allowed time, number and type of obstacles, and their height.

The levels also have parameters for competitors with regard to age, experience (as defined by previous completion of other horse trials or events), and also, the horse's experience or age.

The one beautifully simple aspect of eventing is the fact that the way a competitor moves up in competition also relates directly to the scoring of the trial or event, and the year-end awards.

Horse trials are the qualifying competitions for those wanting to compete at an event. By the time your child is ready, you will indeed be a very seasoned horse show parent, and the USEF rule book for eventing will be ingrained in your file cabinet of knowledge. The levels described here will be for horse trials only. Tests will have their own specific rules, but will be similar to horse trials.

At all levels there are distinctions between Open and Regular divisions. An Open division is typically a professional division that has some age restrictions, but may not have restrictions on the competitor's previous competitions. This allows professionals to bring young horses along in a safe and systematic way. The levels explained below are for youth, although they also apply to amateurs. Always refer to your USEF rule book for more complete information.

The eventing season has a purpose and goal. At levels higher than Training, competitors are trying to qualify for events, so as the season continues, the tests and courses become harder. For Beginner Novice, Novice, and Training levels, the season will offer variety rather than increasing challenges.

All distances and heights are metrically measured. This is a good time to learn what the rest of the world already understands. You will not need to be standing at the arena gate converting fence heights into feet, but we've included the feet and inches of each metric measurement for reference.

Beginner Novice Rider

This is a good starting place, but youngsters who have been to schooling shows or tests may have competed at even lower levels, such as Amoebas and Tadpoles.

Dressage: USEF Novice C test.

Show Jumping: Fence heights to 2'7".

Cross-Country: Obstacles to 2'7", of a simple and inviting variety. No combinations or bullfinches at this level.

Novice

For those who have competed in schooling (non-sanctioned) competitions of some type, and also have experience in all of the three disciplines of dressage, show jumping, and cross-country. The horse must be at least four years old. Competitors can be any age, although the children may sometimes be scored separately from adults. The competitor cannot have completed more than two horse trials at the Training Level in the previous twenty-four months.

Dressage: USEF Novice C and D tests. All dressage tests are available on the USEA's Web site, under the Omnibus section.

Show Jumping: 9 to 11 jumps at a height of no more than .90 m (2'11"). The speed allowed is based on 300 mpm (meters per minute), with the entire length of the course between 350 to 450 meters. Spread (width) of the jumps can be up to 1 meter (or 3'3") at the highest point of the jump. With experience, a rider learns to pace herself to the appropriate speed.

Cross-Country: 16 to 20 jumping efforts over a course of 1,600 to 2,000 meters. The optimum time is 350 to 400 mpm, with a speed fault limit at 470 mpm. Heights are .90 m (2'11"), and spreads can be up to 1.00 m (3'3"). Drops are up to 1.20 m (3'11").

Training Novice Rider

For those with a little more experience and the desire to move up, this level is a little more difficult than Novice, but the courses are still straightforward and encouraging. The competitor may not have competed at more than two horse trials at the Preliminary Level in the previous twenty-four months.

Dressage: Training Level tests C and D.

Show Jumping: 10 to 12 jumping efforts at a height of 1.00 meter (3'3"). Speed allowed is 325 mpm, with spreads being up to 1.15 m (3'9") at the highest point.

Cross-Country: 20 to 24 efforts, obstacle heights of 1 meter (3'3"); brush heights can be up to 1.20 meters (3'11"). Length of course is 2,000 to 2,400 meters (roughly a mile and a half) at an optimum time of 420 to 470 mpm (about 16 mph), with the speed fault limit being 520 mpm. Spreads to be jumped without height (such as water) can be 7'11" wide, and spreads of obstacle can be up to 1.20 meters (4'). Drops can be 1.4 m (4'7").

Preliminary

This is the stepping-stone to One (★) Star Three-Day Events for both horse and rider. The jumps are higher, the dressage more exacting, and all phases are more technically oriented. The competitors must be at least fourteen years old, and the horse must be at least five years old. The competitor must have completed four horse trials at Training Level or higher, but not more than two at the Intermediate Level or higher during the previous twenty-four months.

Dressage: Preliminary tests C and D.

Show Jumping: 11 to 13 jumping efforts at a speed of 350 mpm. Heights are 1.10 m (3'7"), with 1.30 m (4'3") the limit for the spreads.

Cross-Country: 24 to 28 jumping efforts over a course of 2,200 to 2,800 meters at an optimum time of 520 mpm (19⅜ mph). There are no speed faults at this level and above. The spreads can be up to 1.30 m (4'3"). Drops are up to 1.60 m (5'3").

Intermediate

Higher, harder, and a preparation for Two (★★) Star Three-Day Events, these are serious competitors looking for a national spot. Riders must be at least sixteen years old (see page 174) and the horse must be at least six years old. Both competitor and horse must have completed four horse trials at the Preliminary Level or higher. It is not necessary that they completed these as a team. The rider must not have competed more than twice (in the previous twenty-four months) at the Advanced Level, although this restriction does not apply to the horse.

Dressage: Intermediate tests D and E.

Show Jumping: 12 to 14 jumping efforts with heights up to 1.20 m (3'11"). The course is 400 to 500 meters in length with a speed of 350 mpm. The spreads can be up to 1.45 m (4'9").

Cross-Country: 28 to 32 jumping efforts over 2,600 to 3,200 meters (nearly 2 miles) at a speed of 550 mpm. The spreads can be 1.45 m (4'9"). Drops are up to 1.80 m (5'11").

Advanced

Big, bold, and bold-moving are the terms to define this level. The jumps and obstacles are big, the movement in dressage is bold, as is the rider. This prepares the horse and/or rider for Three (★★★) and Four (★★★★) Star Three-Day Events. The rider must be at least eighteen years old and the horse six years old. They both must have completed four horse trials at the Intermediate Level, either together, or in another horse/rider combination. This division is for horse and rider combinations that are on an Olympic hopeful track.

Dressage: Advanced tests C and D.

Show Jumping: 13 to 15 jumping efforts at a speed of 375 mpm. The maximum height is 1.3 m (4'3"), and the spreads are 1.60 m (5'3").

Cross-Country: This course is 3,000 to 3,800 meters at 570 mpm. There are 32 to 40 jumping efforts with heights up to 1.20 m (3'11"), and spreads of 1.80 m (5'11"). Drops are up to 2.00 m (6'7").

THE SCORING

Every keen horse show parent wants to know about the scoring. After all, how much fun is it to muck stalls and traipse around in the rain if we can't measure our own value by the ribbons our child takes home?! All kidding aside, eventing scores are easy to figure, but can often be confusing upon closer examination.

First of all, it's important to remember that all the scores are combined for an overall total. Your daughter may be in last place after one test, but two more very well-done phases can boost her back up into the ribbons . . . or vice versa. The second point to remember is that the lowest score wins. Not quite what we're used to in sports, but that's how it's done in eventing. Here's how it works:

Cross-Country Scoring
(USEF Article 1741)

As with show jumping, the object is to jump all of the obstacles on the course in the correct order, within the time allowed, but not too fast. The lowest score wins. Faults include those at obstacles, such as running out, refusing or circling (see the USEF rule for a complete understanding), and falls of horse or competitor. Other faults are time and speed faults, plus other particular competitor errors that would result in elimination. Penalties are given as follows:

OBSTACLE FAULTS ARE CATEGORIZED IN TWO WAYS:
Disobediences
- 20 points for first refusal, circle, or run-out
- 40 points for the second disobedience at the same obstacle
- Elimination for the third disobedience at the same obstacle

Falls
- 65 points—first fall of competitor
- Elimination—second fall of competitor
- Mandatory retirement—first fall of horse

TIME AND SPEED FAULTS
Time Faults
- 0.4 points per second over optimum time
- Elimination—for exceeding time *limit* (Remember that time limit is the longest time allowed, and optimum time is the ideal.)

Speed Faults (For Novice and Training levels only)

- To discourage unsafe and reckless speed at the lower levels, a penalty of 0.4 points are given for each second under the Speed Fault Time

Other reasons for elimination, listed under USEF Article 1741.3, include improper head gear and tack, failure to stop when signaled, willfully blocking an overtaking competitor or endangering another competitor, jumping the obstacles in the wrong direction, and omitting an obstacle.

Show Jumping Scoring
(USEF Article 1747)

Penalty points will be given as follows:

- **Time faults:** 1 point per second (or fraction of a second) over the optimum time, up to the time limit (Over the limit is an elimination.)
- **Jump faults:** 4 points per rail down
  - 4 points for first disobedience, such as a refusal
  - 8 points for second disobedience
  - 8 points for first fall of a rider
  - Elimination for third disobedience, fall of a horse, second fall of a rider

Some instances have more complicated scoring, such as when there is a knockdown and a refusal. There are many other variables, particularly in the cross-country test, so keep your thumb on your rule book, take some ginkgo, and then remember someone else is keeping the score, even if you aren't.

Dressage Scoring
(USEF Article 1736)

This is where calculators seem to be the best invention of all time. Each individual required movement in a dressage test, in addition to what are called "collective marks," are awarded a "good" point from 0 to 10. A "sufficient" performance is given five points, so every point slides up and down according to how sufficient (or good) or how insufficient (or bad) the performance of each movement was judged to be. Zero is given if the movement was not performed. The tests can be found online at www.usea.com.

"Errors of Course" (going off course) are penalized by subtracting the following points:

- First Error—2 points
- Second Error—4 points
- Third Error—Elimination

All the good marks are added to collective marks, then any penalty points (above) are deducted. That total is now divided by the total possible good marks, multiplied by 100, and rounded to two decimal digits. This is then subtracted from 100, and the resulting score is the score in penalty points for the test. Whew! Who would have guessed you'd need a slide rule at a horse show?

For example:

$$106 \text{ good marks}$$
$$-2 \text{ (one test or course error)}$$
$$+24 \text{ collective marks}$$
$$128 \text{ Total out of 200 possible good marks}$$
$$128/200 = .64 \times 100 = 64.00$$
$$100 - 64.00 = 36.00$$

Scoring is definitely complicated, but it's easy to see that in an eventing dressage test, the highest number of "good" marks always results in the lowest score, thus putting the lowest scorer back in the winner's circle. If there is more than one judge, judges' scores are added together and divided by the number of judges, resulting in an "average."

Most events will have boards posting all the scores for the day and for the previous days so you can keep an eye on your child's placing. Placings at events go to year-end awards, and also to eligibility for the next levels of competition, a very systematic way to keep competitors—children and adults alike—competing at safe levels. Seventy-five percent of all amateur eventers compete at Novice and Training levels, and that's part of what makes the sport so fun. One need not advance if one doesn't feel safe, or one's horse is only suited to the lower levels, and there will always be plenty of jolly good company. But for the keen, ambitious competitor, following the path to higher jumps and greater glory is available and accessible, while still preserving the option to step down to a lower level if necessary.

Moving Up

The rules for advancing are stated in the levels sections, but for a quick recap, here are the ages and qualifications for juniors and amateurs participating in Horse Trials (rules for tests and three-day events may vary):

Novice: Any age; may not have completed more than two horse trials at Training Level in the previous twenty-four months.

Training: Any age; may not have completed more than two horse trials at Preliminary Level or higher in the previous twenty-four months.

Preliminary: At least fourteen years old (see calendar year, page 174); must have completed four horse trials at Training Level or higher, but may not have completed more than two at Intermediate Level or higher in the previous twenty-four months.

Intermediate: At least sixteen years old; must have completed four horse trials at Preliminary Level or higher, but may not have completed more than two at Preliminary Level or higher in the previous twenty-four months.

Advanced: At least eighteen years old; must have completed four horse trials at the Intermediate Level or higher.

POINTS

The USEA has a point system for grading competing event horses, and this system is also used for giving year-end awards to riders. However, there is a different system for adult and youth amateurs who are competing at the Novice and Training levels. The points are based on the overall placing at recognized competitions, and are based on the number of competitors participating. For further information, see Appendix III on page 239.

YEAR-END AWARDS

At every level, there will be a year-end award for Novice Level and up for a rider in her own age group. The top-ranking national rider will get the first place award. The top ten will be noted on the USEA's "Leader Board," found on their Web site. For example, a child who competes and does well at the Novice Level will have a shot at the year-end award. In addition, she may be invited to compete at the American Eventing Championship, inaugurated in North Carolina in September 2004. Check the USEA Web site (www.useventing.com) for the current "Leader Board." (Click on "Competitions," then go to "Leader Board.")

Each region will also have its own year-end placements; see your area's Web site for rules and qualifications. The areas are as follows:

Area I: Connecticut, Maine, Massachusetts, New Hampshire, New York, Rhode Island, and Vermont

Area II: New Jersey, Eastern Pennsylvania, Maryland, Delaware, Virginia, and North Carolina

Area III: Tennessee, South Carolina, Mississippi, Alabama, Georgia, Eastern Louisiana, and Florida

Area IV: Illinois, Iowa, Kansas, Missouri, Minnesota, Nebraska, North Dakota, and Wisconsin

Area V: Arkansas, western half of Louisiana, Oklahoma, and Texas

Area VI: California and Hawaii

Area VII: Oregon, Washington, Idaho, Montana, and Alaska

Area VIII: Indiana, Kentucky, Michigan, Ohio, Western Pennsylvania, and West Virginia

Area IX: Colorado, Wyoming, Utah, Montana, South Dakota, and Idaho

Area X: Arizona, New Mexico, and Nevada

NATIONAL COMPETITIONS

The North American Young Riders Championship

The North American Young Riders Championship (NAYRC) is an inter-disciplinary event for competitors in the Olympic equestrian discipline of eventing, dressage, and show jumping, and also reining. The riders are ages sixteen to twenty-one, and have all been competing close to the top level of their sport. It is a sponsored program that allows young riders to compete against the best in North America: Canada, Mexico, Bermuda, and certain Caribbean Islands in an Olympic-style competition. Each USEA area sends four teams to this event, held each August. Information about this competition can be found on the USEA's Web site: www.useventing.com.

American Eventing Championship

New in the fall of 2004, the American Eventing Championship is a year-end horse trial that showcases the nation's best competitors at all levels, an exciting Olympic type competition that riders must qualify for in their individual levels, Novice through Advanced. The championship takes place at the Carolina Horse Park in Raeford, North Carolina, over four days at the end of September. The event is filled with fun activities for riders and spectators, and awards numerous cash prizes, trophies, saddles, and other prizes for the winners.

QUALIFYING CRITERIA

In order to participate, riders must qualify at their level during the qualifying period of the first Tuesday in August of the previous year to the first Tuesday in August of the current year of the championship.

The qualifications are valid only for USEA-recognized competitions and USEA-recognized Area Championships. Qualifying wins count for each level only.

Novice Division:	Place 1st through 3rd at one Novice Horse Trial or 1st–5th in an Area Championship
Training Division:	Place 1st through 3rd at one Training Horse Trial or 1st–5th in an Area Championship
Preliminary Division:	Place 1st through 3rd at one Preliminary Horse Trial or 1st–5th in an Area Championship or 1st–5th in any CIC★ 1st–6th in any CCI★
Intermediate Division:	1st through 3rd at one Intermediate Horse Trial or 1st–5th in any Area Championship or 1st–5th in any CIC★★ 1st–6th in any CCI★★
Advanced Division:	1st–6th at one Advanced Horse Trial 1st–10th at any Area Championship 1st–8th at any CIC★★★ 1st–10th at any CCI★★★ 1st–20th at any CCI★★★★

Young Rider Program

The USEA offers a Young Riders Program to all riders twenty-one and under through each of the ten USEA areas. Educational and rider development activities are offered, such as camps, clinics, and seminars featuring the top competitors in the sport. Fund-raising is done in each area for these activities, and money is raised to send the top competitors to the NAYRC (North American Young Riders Championship) and the European Young Riders Championship.

EVENTING RESOURCES

Web Sites

www.chronofhorse: Web site for the weekly magazine, *The Chronicle of the Horse*, containing results and news and commentary of interest for those in hunter/jumpers, dressage, and eventing.

www.equisearch.com: Equestrian Web site parented by Primedia Publications, publisher of *Practical Horseman* and other equestrian magazines.

www.usef.org: The United States Equestrian Federation Web site has the official rules for eventing, plus much more about the sport, and national and international equestrian news.

www.useventing.com: The United States Eventing Association (USEA) Web site with links to each Area Web site (see below). Each area chapter is a great resource for young riders, helping them to advance by offering events, scholarships and clinics.

USEA AREA WEB SITES

www.area1usea.org Area I: Connecticut, Maine, Massachusetts, New Hampshire, New York, Rhode Island, and Vermont

www.usea2.net Area II: New Jersey, Eastern Pennsylvania, Maryland, Delaware, Virginia, and North Carolina

www.area3.addr.com Area III: Alabama, Florida, Georgia, Eastern Louisiana, Mississippi, South Carolina, and Tennessee

www.uscta4.org Area IV: Illinois, Iowa, Kansas, Missouri, Minnesota, Nebraska, North Dakota, and Wisconsin

www.area5online.com Area V: Arkansas, Louisiana (western half), Oklahoma, and Texas www.areavi.org Area VI: California and Hawaii

www.areavii.org Area VII: Alaska, Idaho, Oregon, Montana, and Washington

www.usea8.org: Area VIII: Indiana, Kentucky, Michigan, Ohio, Western Pennsylvania, and West Virginia

www.msea–usea.org Area IX (Mountain States): Colorado, Wyoming, Utah, Montana, South Dakota, and Idaho

www.usea-areax.com Area X: Arizona, New Mexico, and Nevada

Books

The United States Pony Club Manual of Horsemanship: Basics for Beginners/ D Level by editors Susan E. Harris and Ruth Ring Harvie (Howell Reference Books).

A Young Person's Guide to Eventing by Gill Watson (Pony Club).

Practical Eventing by Sally O'Connor.

Eventing USA magazine, published by the USEA and available as part of a yearly membership.

CHAPTER

12

It's Not Soccer

As any parent knows, raising children is a complex and expensive process. Raising a child who loves horses brings greater complexity and expense to the arena (no pun intended). Going forward in this millennium, we are faced with rapid-fire changes in technology that are constantly affecting our lives and our lifestyles. And for all the so-called ease of life that advanced technology is supposed to bring, we constantly find ourselves more hurried, more harried, more overworked and tired. As parents, when our child loves horses, we are at first taken aback and then pleased on some deep subliminal level that our child has dragged us into this world where time has stopped and the language becomes one of smells and whinnies and warmth. It's wholesome. It's different from our everyday lives. And, yes, as we already know, it's expensive.

Equestrian sport is not a hobby where you need to scrape together forty dollars for soccer shoes; its expenses are prohibitive to most of the population. A horse's shoes cost way more than soccer shoes, and horses get new ones every other month (they also lose them as easily as any eight-year-old child). Winter blankets for horses that are in training cost more than most people's dress coats. Feed and bedding, supplements, tack, and those ever-present vet bills make keeping a horse an astronomical affair. I know that there isn't a parent out there who does not struggle with the issue of horses and money, even though there is a huge sliding scale of economy.

There are families who give up vacations and dinners out to keep one horse or pony for their child. There are others who struggle to attend a few horse shows a year, and still others who have the means to have several horses showing all over their region, and sometimes, the nation. But even these families must have issues about the expense and the message the expense is sending to their child.

I've met physicians who muck stalls for their kids, working students who groom at shows just for the chance to be there, and parents from all walks of life and professions who just simply love their kids to death and somehow make it all work.

It's not easy. I occasionally wake up in the middle of the night and ask myself, "Am I nuts?" When Chétie started showing regularly, I was a full-time nursing student. When we would go to a horse show, it was usually Thursday night after I'd been in clinicals all day—from a 4:30 A.M. wake-up call, followed by a ten-hour day (including driving). I would then come home at 3:00 P.M., hitch up the trailer, get the pony, and head off on a four-hour ride to Kansas City or St. Louis. My mantra was "I *must* be nuts!" My mother thought so. Most of my friends thought so too, and some were eager to tell me that what I did was disproportionate to what any mother should do for a child. But I know that Chétie, who as my youngest child was eleven years old at the time, would grow up in a way that would seem no longer than the turning of one season. All those hours in the truck would be precious memories for her, and also for me. And in this, as a parent, I also know that I'm not alone.

I believed then (and I still do) that the time we structure around a sport with our kids gives us a venue for communication that would otherwise not happen in our cell phone, Web-driven world. There are so many of life's lessons that can be learned, and so many ways that a parent can observe the success of those lessons, when you're dealing with animals. And this is especially true with horses, those wonderful creatures that require both our command and our delicacy of handling. In addition, the interactions of child and trainer, child and peers, and child and competitors also teach lessons of manners, respect, kindness, helpfulness, love, tenderness, and self-reflection. There are the lessons learned in competition: pride (but not too much), success with humility, failure with dignity, self-understanding, and gratitude for life's opportunities.

As a parent, I feel very fortunate that we've been able to give our child this opportunity of a life involved with horses. And while I always worry over the expense and struggle to put it into the big perspective of our family budget—a seemingly impossible task compared with other sports—I think of the world Chétie is growing up in, and how the opportunity to spend those years with her pony, and now with her horse (and the other horses in the barn), will give her a foundation that is, in my view, priceless.

I think of all the days she spends at the barn instead of aimlessly wandering around with her friends or watching television. I think of her beaming pride when she finally learned to groom her pony with some skill, and then body-clip her horse, wrap him for shipping, tend to his cuts, and keep a sharp eye for any changes that would mean he wasn't feeling just right. I think of her mental development when I watched her figure out her distances to the jump—watching, waiting, holding, pressing forward—and the confidence it gave her after such a long sought-after accomplishment, one which she worked on for years.

I saw her give remarkable concentrated attention to holding her still-green pony straight so that she wouldn't swap her lead. I saw the way that the older kids in the barn treated her with such sweetness, and how they cheered her successes, and how she looked up to them with respect for their accomplishments. And in all of this I saw a child developing qualities which would guide her through this new century with grace and dignity and self-purpose, unafraid to reach out for life's successes and undeterred by its failures.

Now, maybe we could have gotten this with soccer, but I don't think so.

Note: "It's Not Soccer" appeared in a slightly different form in the November 2000 issue of *Practical Horseman*.

Appendix I A: American Quarter Horse Association (AQHA)

The American Quarter Horse Association is the original and largest of the Western breeds. Most other Western breeds generally base their rules for showing on the AQHA's handbook. If your child starts with the Quarters (as they are affectionately referred to), you will be able to easily navigate any change to other breeds. Only points and awards for the classes listed in Chapter 8 will be covered, although there are many other ways to compete in the Quarters. For sanctioned shows, points are earned in each class or division based on the number of competitors and the placing as follows:

AQHA Rule 415a

Place→ Number of entries↓	1	2	3	4	5	6	7	8	9	10
3–4	½									
5–9	1	½								
10–14	2	1	½							
15–19	3	2	1	½						
20–24	4	3	2	1	½					
25–29	5	4	3	2	1	½				
30–34	6	5	4	3	2	1	½			
35–39	7	6	5	4	3	2	1	½		
40–44	8	7	6	5	4	3	2	1	½	
45 & up	9	8	7	6	5	4	3	2	1	½

Some shows have two judges, and are referred to as a "double-judged show." In this case, each judge pins each class independently of the other judge. In practical terms, this means your child will receive two sets of points. Conceivably, she could get a 1st place and 3rd place, or some other combination, depending on what each judge sees and prefers about her horse or her performance.

Young riders can compete in the Novice or Youth divisions. The Novice division is for inexperienced riders just new to showing who have not earned a lot of points at the recognized shows. Once a rider has earned ten or more combined points in regular youth or open performance classes (except for halter), she is no longer eligible to compete as a novice. The American Quarter Horse Youth Association (AQHYA) has nice cumulative awards for this division, with a buckle award to the novice who accumulates forty points over time, and also a Rookie of the Year award for the high-point novice rider of the year.

There are three big awards at each show that the AQHYA sponsors:

1. **Grand Champion:** This is awarded to the best horse at halter. There may be many different horses exhibited by youth exhibitors, based on the age and sex of the horse. A bronze trophy is awarded the first time your child's horse wins this award. After that you may purchase one each time the award is won (Rule 417).

2. **All Around Trophy:** A bronze trophy is given (again, for the first time, as above) for the high-point earner in a combination of events and categories (see Rule 417c). Scoring for the All Around Trophy is a little more complicated than the simple points system. Each competitor placing in the top nine is given a "credit" for each competitor placing below them, plus an extra "credit." Halter credits are a little different. Rule 417F will become a well-thumbed part of your rule book. After your child wins the first All Around Trophy on her horse, the AQHYA issues special certificates for each subsequent win. If your child competes and wins on another horse, then she can win the trophy again (Rule 419).

3. **Superior All-Around:** This is a title awarded to those talented (and busy) horse/rider competitors who have earned fifty or more all-around titles (Rule 421).

In addition to the awards above, a particular horse show may also offer other prizes. Local clubs may offer fun prizes at the horse show in addition to a series award for a particular season. It makes showing all the more fun, and is also rewarding to those kids who can't travel to compete far from home.

AQHA YOUTH WORLD SHOW

The biggest show for kids showing in the Quarters is held once a year, open by invitation only to those competitors earning the following points during the year:

*Yearling Mares-1.5	*Yearling geldings-1
*2-year-old mares-4	*2-year-old geldings-6
*3-year-old mares-7	*3-year-old geldings-6
*Aged mares-14.5	*Aged geldings-22
Western Pleasure-37	Trail-23
Working Hunter-8.5	Hunter Under Saddle-35
Hunter Hack-11	Hunt Seat Equitation-23
Showmanship-38	Western Horsemanship-36
Barrel Racing-20	Pole Bending-12.5
Jumping-1	Western Riding-15
Reining-10.5	Equitation over Fences-5.5

* Halter classes

LIFETIME ACHIEVEMENTS

Youth horse/rider combinations can accumulate points toward awards over the years. For as long as your youngster is riding the same horse, she can accumulate points toward these awards. Once the horse is sold to another rider, the horse keeps the points, but your child starts over. The award categories are outlined in Rule 422. The award rules are noted below:

- **AQHA Register of Merit (ROM):** Awarded to youth horse/rider combination with at least 10 points for halter and performance events. For performance events, at least 5 points must be won in a specific category (Rule 423).
- **AQHA Versatility Award:** This one requires 65 points spread over 8 events with at least 10 points earned in 5 different events, and 5 points in each of the other 3 events. This rewards a well-rounded combination (Rule 424).

- **AQHA Champion:** This requires 35 points won in at least 5 shows, under 5 different judges, with at least 15 points from halter and 15 from performance. Whew, better read the rule! (Rule 424).
- **AQHA Supreme Champion:** 50 points, 15 in halter (8 of these points must have been earned when the horse was 2 years old), 5 points each in 4 different performance categories, with the remaining 15 spread out over performance or halter (Rule 427).
- **AQHA Superior (Event) Horse:** 50 points in any one particular event (Rule 428).
- **AQHA Performance Champion:** This is awarded to that lucky youth who has earned three of the above.
- **AQHA Supreme Performance Champion:** Six Superior Horse awards makes this award Supreme.

Appendix I B: American Paint Horse Association (APHA)

At an American Paint Horse Show, there will be one point awarded for every three horses judged in a class, for up to a total of twelve points and eighteen horses. The points are given per judge—meaning, if there are two judges, there are two sets of points. The points are *not* averaged, because each judge may place the class in a different order.

There are two basic rules, and these will become clearer as we define them below. The rules are:

1. Points are awarded based on the number of competitors in a class.
2. For each judge judging the class, the points are given as in rule number one. The points are not merely multiplied by the number of judges, as each judge will award his/her own points. It can happen that in a class of eighteen, twelve competitors could get points because each judge picked a different group for the top six spots. If there are three judges, all eighteen competing could happen to get points and ribbons, although this is less likely.

The events for youth competitors may be divided into two age groups:
- Ages thirteen and under
- Ages fourteen through eighteen

The chart below is an example of the point system for APHA.

Place→	1	2	3	4	5	6
# of horses↓						
3	1	0	0	0	0	0
6	2	1	0	0	0	0
9	3	2	1	0	0	0
12	4	3	2	1	0	0
15	5	4	3	2	1	0
18	6	5	4	3	2	1

Rule SC–060

A class with eighteen horses is called a "full point" class. Classes with more than eighteen maintain the same points as for the eighteen. So, in practical terms, if your daughter competed in a Horsemanship class (ages 14 to 18) and came in first out of twelve, she would receive four points toward a year-end award for that particular class. Each state may also have its own awards, in addition to national and zone awards. Plus, if she wins or places in other classes, she may win an overall "high point" award for her age division for that particular show. This high point award may come with some fun tangible evidence, such as a trophy belt or other item to take home.

The larger the show, the more judges there will be to judge it. Parents of kids going for the top twenty national spots will search out the shows with more judges, as these shows earn more points.

Champion: Given to the competitor with the most points for her particular age division at each show. Each individual show may give other trophies as well.

All-Around: For the youth competitor with the most points overall. That is, if your child competed in a lot of events in the 14 to 18 division, her total number of points would go to an "all-around" award.

LIFETIME ACHIEVEMENTS

The APHA, like the other disciplines, offers cumulative awards and titles to those eligible horse/rider combinations that earn points over the youth rider's career. The qualifying events for these awards are outlined in Rules YP-085 and YP-090. Another reason to become familiar with the rule book!

- **APHA Youth Register of Merit (ROM):** This is a title awarded to either a youth or youth/horse combination for earning at least 10 points in any one event. The APHA office will award a certificate for this achievement (Rule YP-050).
- **APHA Youth Performance Versatility Award:** Given to a youth horse/rider combination who earns five ROMs with at least one of those in Showmanship at Halter (Rule YP-040).
- **APHA Youth Superior Event Award:** This title is awarded to the youth horse/rider combination who has earned at least 50 points in any one of the approved events (Rule YP-045).

These "lifetime achievements" can be earned for youth horse/rider combinations as long as the competitor is under eighteen. Once the rider graduates to Amateur status, the points must be earned again for similar awards. These awards can bring great pride in one's horse (and ability in the partnership), but also a good resale value when it is time to move on (or when your child is off to college).

Appendix I C: Appaloosa Horse Club (ApHC)

The Appaloosa Youth Association (AYA) is the junior organization for the ApHC. Its members and governance are youth members, those eighteen years and younger. (See age rule, page 174.)

A youth may compete in open divisions, but only points earned in the youth classes will count toward national year-end youth awards. A few basic rules are as follows:

1. One must be a member of the AYA in order for points to count.
2. The youth must own the horse ridden in competition in order to accrue points.
3. Only one horse per youth class is allowed per exhibitor, but a youth may ride another horse in a different class. Any horse ridden by the youth must be properly registered with ApHC.

Points are based on the number of horses judged in the particular class. The judge must place to 8th (if available), but only the top seven accrue points.

Place→	1	2	3	4	5	6	7
# of horses↓							
2	½						
3–7	1	½					
8–12	2	1	½				
13–17	3	2	1	½			
18–22	4	3	2	1	½		
23–27	5	4	3	2	1	½	
28 +	6	5	4	3	2	1	½

Rule 701

Placings at the Horse Show will be based on points earned. A high-point award is given to the youth with the most points earned overall in youth classes.

YOUTH LIFETIME AWARDS

Refer to Rule 804 for a list of classes in which points accumulate over the life of your child's career. The rules governing these awards are also well covered in that rule, so will not be repeated here. Here is a quick glance at the points needed for these awards—but remember that each award has some specific requirement for which type of classes are eligible for the point totals.

Youth Achievement Roll: 30 points, with at least 10 points each in two categories of Showmanship or Performance (Rule 804 B).

Appaloosa Youth Achievement: 50 points are required, and they must have been earned under at least five different judges; 10 points must have come from Showmanship, 20 from at least two categories of performance (Rule 804 C).

Youth Achievement Champion: 175 points, of which 35 need to be from Showmanship, 70 from Performance, 18 of which were earned in at least 3 different performance sub-categories (Rule 804 D).

Appaloosa Youth Superior Achievement Champion: This requires 350 points from at least 5 different shows and 5 different judges; 105 points need to be earned in Showmanship, with at least 140 in Performance.

Additional awards can be found in Rule 805.

Appendix I D: Pony of the Americas (POAC)

The Pony of the Americas Club sponsors its own shows, and has a system for awarding points for the classes at the shows. That system is outlined below. The POAC also approves POA classes at state fairs and inter-breed shows, and events called Building and Promotion Shows (B & P); the system for those points is covered in Rule 62. Special shows called Pony Rama Shows have two judges, and therefore each class comes with a double set of points. In that instance the judges give points independently of each other. As with every organization, the rider and pony must be current members of the POAC.

The Class A Shows must offer a minimum number of halter and performance classes per Rule 54. For these shows, points are tabulated as follows:

# of competitors→	6	5	4	3	2	1
Place ↓						
1	12	11	10	9	8	7
2	11	10	9	8	7	
3	10	9	8	7		
4	9	8	7			
5	8	7				
6	7					

Rule 58

For halter classes with more than nine competitors, bonus points are awarded as such:

# of Ponies	Bonus Points
10–13	1
14–17	2
18–21	3
22–25	4
26–29	5
30–33	6
34–37	7
38–41	8
42–45	9
46 and up	10

Rule 69A

For performance classes with more than thirteen competitors, the bonus points are awarded as follows:

# of Ponies	Bonus Points
14–21	1
22–29	2
30–37	3
38–45	4
46–53	5
54–61	6
62–69	7
70–77	8
78–85	9
86 and up	10

Rule 69B

LIFETIME ACHIEVEMENT

Register of Merit (ROM): This is similar to the other breeds, and is a cumulative award that rewards the pony (not the rider) for his competitive success over the years. It is based on points earned, and differs slightly based on the type of event in which the points have accumulated (Rule 142).

Supreme Champion: This award is presented to a pony who earns ROMs in four different areas (Rule 142F).

In addition to ROMs, there are many other cumulative awards for classes other than those covered here. There is also a POA horseback riding program that has achievement levels for hours in the saddle, awarding for 50 hours up to 5,000 hours (Rule 151).

Appendix I E: Pinto Horse Association
of America (PtHA)

The PtHAYO is the Pinto Horse Association of America's Youth Organi-zation, which governs the eligibility and rules for youth members. Youth members may earn points toward year-end awards for their horses as well as for their own performance. The points are tabulated as follows:

Place→	1	2	3	4	5	6
# of entries↓						
3	1	0	0	0	0	0
4	2	1	0	0	0	0
5	3	2	1	0	0	0
6	4	3	2	1	0	0
7	5	4	3	2	1	0
8 or more	6	5	4	3	2	1

Rule 59

Except at the Pinto World Show and Area Championships, no points are awarded for classes with fewer than three entries. Points can be earned by the horse, or a horse/rider combination, but can only be earned at rec-ognized shows in ROM-recognized classes. The designations below can be earned in open, amateur, or youth classes, but only the youth points are defined here.

LIFETIME ACHIEVEMENTS
Register of Merit (Rules 60 and 62): A Register of Merit (ROM) des-ignation is an accumulated award. The horse reserves that designation for his entire career, and continues to earn other significations based on the same type of Register of Merit points. A youth rider receives an ROM based on a horse/rider combination. That is, whenever your child rides his horse or pony, they can earn points together, and these are referred to as

units. Only units earned in youth classes count toward ROMs or other cumulative awards.

Only ROM-pointed classes count for point awards. There are many fun classes for your child to compete in, but she will not be getting points in these, only having a good time. These classes include any combined classes such as "trail and jumping" or "ride and drive," mixed Western and English classes, costume, color classes, YA leadline, and YA walk–trot classes. Any class offered by a horse show that does not follow the PtHA rules is also exempt from ROM points.

The information below is only an overview, and cannot take the place of the official PtHA rule book, which must be your ultimate reference.

1. **Register of Merit:** 30 points and one ROM-qualifying first place win.
2. **Register of Excellence:** 175 points and 3 Rom first places.
3. **Certificate of Ability:** ROMs in each of four separate performance events.
4. **Certificate of Achievement:** ROMs in six separate performance events.
5. **Certificate of Superior Ability:** Register of Excellence in four separate performance, which must include showmanship and equitation.
6. **Certificate of Superior Achievement:** Register of Excellence in 6 separate performances, including showmanship and equitation.
7. **Versatility Award:** 65 points and one first place in either Western or English showmanship, Register of Excellence in any event, ROM in 3 separate events (excluding showmanship and equitation). Two of these have to be under Western equipment and one under English equipment, or vice versa, and have earned a Youth ROM in Stock Seat equitation and either Hunt Seat or Saddle Seat equitation.
8. **PtHA Champion:** 150 points won under five or more different judges; 50 of these points have to be won in either Western or English showmanship alone, 65 points in performance or equitation, at least five first place awards under at least three different judges, and a minimum of three ROMs (with at least one of those in performance or equitation).

9. **PtHA Legion of Merit:** This one is for the very dedicated horse show attendees. The points needed are high (650), and the combinations are complicated. Best to check the Pinto rule book. (By the time your child gets to this and the next 2 levels, you will have had a thousand hours of downtown at horse shows to memorize the rulebook.)

10. **Pinto Supreme Champion:** A whopping 1,000 points earned at (at least) twenty or more shows under thirty-five different judges, with a lot of other caveats.

11. **Superior Performance Pinto:** This pinnacle award is the highest given. For YA units (child and horse), the requirements are eight ROMs and thirty-five first place awards, which must include showmanship and equitation.

Appendix I F: Arabian Horse Association (AHA)

Youth points are accumulated for regional and national shows at Class A-level AHA shows. Young riders may qualify in any class of their age division, as long as that class is offered at the regional and national show. There are three categories for the qualifiers. Most of the youth classes covered in Chapter 8 fall under category two. The following is a basic overview. Some classes may require more or less points.

Regional Championship Qualifying Points for Category 2 (Western pleasure, reigning, trail horse, showmanship, Western horsemanship)

- A first or second place
- A regional champion or regional reserve champion

Other Class Qualifying Points:

The following classes require a first through sixth place (no minimum number of participants in the class):

- Walk-Trot, 10 & under
- Showmanship, 10 & under
- Working Hunter and Hunter Hack
- Jumping
- Reining and Trail require earning one score of 68 or better at a participating horse show

National Championship Qualifying Points

For category two, the following points/championships qualify a rider for the National Show:

- Top five placements at Regional Championships
- One champion or two reserve champions from an AHA horse show
- Two first places or one reserve champion and one first place

Riders in reining or trail may also qualify for Nationals with two scores of 68 or above. The AHA handbook is the best source for up-to-date rules governing all aspects of showing and qualifying for the big horse show. It is available at www.arabianhorses.org.

Appendix II A: Hunter/Jumper Organizations

Some of the memberships that your child may need (in addition to USEF and your state organizations) for participation in various finals and year-end awards are listed below. Membership and contact information is available at their Web sites.

Marshall and Sterling League: Children's and Pony Hunters, Children's Pony and Junior Jumpers, Charles Owen Children's Medal (3'), HBO Junior Medal (3'6"): www.hits.com

NAL (North American League): Pony Jumpers, Children's Hunters, and Jumpers

NHS: The National Horse Show, sponsor of the ASPCA Maclay equitation class: www.nhs.org

USEF: United States Equestrian Federation: www.usef.org

USET (United States Equestrian Team): 3'9" Equitation: www.uset.org or www.usef.org

USHJA: United States Hunter/Jumper Association is a member organization for all of those competing in hunters and jumpers: www.ushja.org

WIHS (Washington International Horse Show): Hunters, Equitation, Jumpers: www.wihs.org

www.ryegate.com: This Web site offers horse show results, and jumper and equitation standings, in addition to online horse show prize lists (for the big shows).

HUNTER POINTS
(USEF ARTICLE 917)

Pony Hunters and Junior Hunters have similar scoring based on the ribbons and the rating and number of competitors. Points for Children's Hunters are always based on the "C" rating and the number of competitors. Championship and Reserve Champion awards are based solely on the ribbon value. The Championship and Reserve Champion are usually won by consistency, rather than by just one blue ribbon, and it could be the child with all yellow (3rds) who edges out a few competitors who might have one blue (1st) and then perhaps a mix of lower ribbons. For example:

Your Child	Child B	Child C
Yellow = 4	Blue = 10	White = 2
Yellow = 4	Red = 6	Green = ½
Yellow = 4	White = 2	Red = 6
Yellow = 4	Green = ½	White = 2
Yellow = 4	Green = ½	Red = 6
Total = 20 points	Total = 19 points	Total = 16½ points
Your child would be Champion; Child B would be Reserve Champion.		

All shows are rated by USEF, according to the number of days of competition, amount of prize money given, and number of classes offered. Every show must post its rating on the prize list.

The following tables are the number of points awarded toward Horse of the Year, a year-end award given by USEF (see page 144). The points calculated are also qualifying points for the various year-end finals, also listed in Chapter 9 and in Appendix II C later in this appendix. The top row of the tables give the number of competitors in the class. The number is determined by those entered at the beginning of the first performance class, regardless of whether someone drops out as the division continues.

"AA" Rated Shows

Competitors→	3–8	9–15	16–25	26+
Place↓				
1	40	50	60	70
2	35	45	55	65
3	30	40	50	60
4	25	35	45	55
5	24	34	44	54
6	23	33	43	53

"A" Rated Shows

Competitors→	3–8	9–15	16–25	26+
Place↓				
1	30	40	50	60
2	25	35	45	55
3	20	30	40	50
4	15	25	35	45
5	14	24	34	44
6	13	23	33	43

"B" Rated Shows

Competitors→	3–8	9–15	16–25	26+
Place↓				
1	20	25	30	40
2	15	20	25	35
3	10	15	20	30
4	5	10	15	25
5	4	5	10	20
6	3	4	5	15

"C" Rated Shows

Competitors→	3–8	9–15	16–25	26+
Place↓				
1	15	20	25	30
2	10	15	20	25
3	5	10	15	20
4	4	5	10	15
5	3	4	5	10
6	2	3	4	5

There are two additional items that will jump the point totals:

Champion or Reserve Champion Status: The competitors with the highest and second-highest scores for the division (according to ribbon points) are rewarded with some bonus points. Here's how it works:

- **Champion:** Whatever the value (according to show rating and number of competitors) for first place, in the first class of the division, the value is multiplied by two and added to the points. For instance, at an "AA" show with twelve competitors in the first class, the bonus would be 100 points.

- **Reserve Champion:** The same value is multiplied by 1.2, so for the same example (twelve competitors in the first class at an "AA" show), the bonus would be 60 points.

Hunter Classic: A Hunter Classic is a separate class from the Hunter Division (whether it is Ponies, Children's, Junior's, or Amateur). Hunter Classics are not held at every show, but when they are, it's a beautiful thing to watch. Most kids wear shadbellys, although they are not required to, except for year-end finals. The top twelve riders (if there are twelve) are called back at the end of the hunter rounds. In some cases, the last round of the hunter division is often the first qualifying round for the Classic. That round is given a numerical score, as is the Classic round itself. It is possible to be champion of the division and not place in the Classic. Hunter classics have their own scoring rules, and points are awarded to 12th place. (The scoring is based on 100 percent being perfect—the most rare of scores—with average scores in the 70s, very good in the 80s, and 90s reserved for very exceptional rounds.)

HUNTER CLASSIC POINTS

All rated shows have the same base points for the Hunter Classic, but "A" and "AA" shows have multipliers that increase the points. For "A" shows, multiply the bonus by 4, and for "AA", multiply the bonus by 5. The chart below gives the total values.

Place→ Rating↓	1	2	3	4	5	6	7	8	9	10	11	12
B and C	20	16	14	12	10	8	6	5	4	3	2	1
A	80	64	56	48	40	32	24	20	16	12	81	4
AA	100	80	70	60	50	40	35	25	20	15	10	5

Feel free to copy the scorekeepers on the following page. It will help you keep track.

HUNTER POINT KEEPERS

Class→	1	2	3	4	5	Points
Place ↓						
★1						
2						
3						
4						
5						
6						
★Champion	Value =	2 × 1ˢᵗ	Class 1ˢᵗ	Place	Value =	
★Res. Ch.	Value =	1.2 × 1ˢᵗ	Class 1ˢᵗ	Place	Value =	
Hunter	Classic	Bonus	Points		Value =	
					Total Points→	

Class→	1	2	3	4	5	Points
Place ↓						
★1						
2						
3						
4						
5						
6						
★Champion	Value =	2 × 1ˢᵗ	Class 1ˢᵗ	Place	Value =	
★Res. Ch.	Value =	1.2 × 1ˢᵗ	Class 1ˢᵗ	Place	Value =	
Hunter	Classic	Bonus	Points		Value =	
					Total Points→	

EQUITATION POINTS
(USEF RULE XXII)

The age-specific equitation classes do not count toward any USEF year-end national or zone awards, but your local state organization may have these. Points will be based on the ribbons earned. All other equitation points that are qualifiers for an indoor or national competition are covered in Appendix II C (page 227).

Here is a handy chart to keep track of your child's equitation points.

HORSE SHOW	DATE	CLASS	HOW MANY	PLACE	POINTS

JUMPER POINTS
(USEF RULE XXVII)

As with the other divisions, awards at horse shows are determined by the placing in each class, with Champion and Reserve Champion going to the top two riders.

For USEF, the point tabulation system is the same for both Pony and Children's Jumpers, based on number of exhibitors and placing. It is exactly the same chart as for the "C" rated hunters. Pony Jumpers accumulate points for both Zone and National Horse of the Year Award (HOTYA). Children's Jumpers accumulate points for a Zone HOTYA, but each zone has their own way of tabulating the points. So, it's best to check out your zone's rules at the USEF Web site, www.usef.org.

Children's and Pony Jumper Points

Competitors→	3–8	9–15	16–25	26+
Place↓				
1	15	20	25	30
2	10	15	20	25
3	5	10	15	20
4	4	5	10	15
5	3	4	5	10
6	2	3	4	5

Pony Jumpers are invited by each zone to compete as a team at the year-end Pony Finals. The qualifications for the invitation are, again, specific to each zone.

Pony and Children's Jumpers are invited to the NAL (North American League) championship held in conjunction with the Pennsylvania National Horse Show. Membership in the NAL is necessary, and the qualifications for invitation should be checked with the NAL at www.ryegate.com. Points awarded for NAL Children's Jumper Classics held at horse shows are different from those awarded for HOTYA, points being awarded to at least eight places.

Junior and Young Rider Jumpers accumulate points for every dollar won in their particular division during the year. This may be the easiest record keeping in your Horse Show Mom career! The high-point jumpers can be checked at www.usef.org (click on points). USEF awards HOTYA to the highest-earning junior jumper horse.

The big indoor shows are the goal for the top competitors across the country, whether pony or horse, child or teenager, amateur adult or professional. Points from your child's fifteen most successful horse shows are submitted, and the competitors are drawn from that lot. For all of these shows, the rider must apply even before she knows whether she's qualified, and invitations are only issued to those competitors who have applied. Once the top cut-off numbers are invited, the next riders down the list will be issued invitations if any top riders decline to attend.

THE PENNSYLVANIA NATIONAL HORSE SHOW

Held in October every year in Harrisburg, Pennsylvania, the PNHS offers finals to hunters, jumpers, and USEF Medal finalists. The qualifying year is October 2 through October 1. You must send an application with a deposit, which will be refunded to you if your child does not make the cut.

Hunters

Approximately thirty of the top Junior Hunters and Pony Hunters are invited to compete. In addition, the top twenty-five Children's Hunters in the NAL (North American League) are also invited to compete (see hunter points in Appendix II B, page 219).

Equitation

The USEF Medal final, the goal of many junior equitation riders, is open by invitation to all of those riders who qualify during the year by earning points in the USEF Medal class at rated horse shows. There is only one USEF Medal class per horse show, and the number of points earned in each Medal class is based on the number of entries:

USEF Medal Points

# of Competitors→	6–15	16–30	30+
Place↓			
1	10	20	30
2	6	12	18
3	4	8	12
4	2	4	6

Note: All classes over fifty will be divided into two separately judged classes.

The points required for entry to the year-end final are based on the state of your permanent residence. Points from any horse show hosting a USEF Medal class count, even if you participate outside your state.

Here are the points required for each state:

60 Points:	CT, NJ, NY
38 Points:	FL, MA, PA, RI
25 Points:	CA, DE, GA, IA, IL, MD, MN, NC, NE, ND, NV, OH, OK, SC, SD, TN, VA, WI
13 Points:	All other states not listed above, plus Canada and Puerto Rico

For example: If you live in New York, your child will have to win sixty points, either by getting lots of top-four ribbons at small shows, or winning two firsts at really big shows. Somebody always does it. If you live in Missouri, she will only have to accrue thirteen points. The Pennsylvania National Horse Show usually hosts two hundred or more Junior Equitation riders every year (256 competed in 2004).

Jumpers

Pony and Children's Jumpers are invited to the NAL (North American League) championship held in conjunction with the Pennsylvania National Horse Show. Membership in the NAL is necessary, and the qualifications for invitation should be checked with the NAL at www.ryegate.com. Points awarded for NAL Children's Jumper Classics held at horse shows are different from those awarded for HOTYA, points being awarded to at least eight places.

- **Pony Jumpers:** 25 pony/rider combinations are issued invitations, but you must first apply.
- **NAL Children's Jumpers:** 25 of the top horse/rider combinations are accepted (out of those that apply).
- **Prix des States:** Junior Jumper teams chosen by each zone. The top four junior jumper riders from each zone are invited to participate as a team. Each zone has its own selection criteria, so check on USEF's Web site for your zone's specifications.

THE NATIONAL HORSE SHOW

Held in November every year, there are two National Horse Shows: one in New York City, and the other a few weeks later in Wellington, Florida.

Hunters

Pony Hunters and Junior Hunters are invited based on their national standing. Usually only the top ten to twenty are invited, and they may go to one or both shows.

Equitation

The ASPCA Maclay Final is held at the New York National Horse Show every year. The points awarded in each class are based on the same residence and class-size requirements as the USEF Medal. The difference is this: Once qualified, the equitation rider must compete at a regional final to then earn a spot at the national final. Approximately 100 of the nation's top riders earn a seat at the Metropolitan National Horse Show for the Maclay Medal, and the number invited from each region is based on a ratio of competitors from all the regional finals. For instance, if all of the combined regional finals have 225 competitors, 225 is divided into 100 (the number invited may change from year to year, but this is an average): $100/225 = .444$. This number is multiplied by the number competing at each regional. If your child's regional final has 20 competitors, then: $20 \times .444 = 8.88$. That means the top 8 competitors at your regional will be invited to the finals. Regional finals with more competitors will obviously have more invited to the finals: $50 \times .444 = 22.2$, so 22 will be invited.

Jumpers

Based on dollars earned, the top jumpers in these divisions are invited to compete:

- Junior Jumpers
- Children's Jumpers (Florida only)

In 2004, thirty junior jumpers were invited to attend the National. These numbers may change from year to year. Keep track of your child's standing online at www.nhs.org.

THE WASHINGTON INTERNATIONAL HORSE SHOW (WIHS)

The WIHS is also held in October or early November every year, following the PNHS. The qualifying year is September 1 through August 31.

Hunters

The top thirty or so are invited in the Junior Hunter, Children's Hunter, and Pony Hunter divisions. Points are based on the best fifteen horse shows in your child's record for the year.

Equitation

This highly competitive final is for the top thirty to thirty-five or so competitors in the nation. Points are earned by being in the top six in the WIHS equitation classes at qualifying shows. Therefore, in order to be in the top thirty nationally, riders need to attend many horse shows, and score many points in this one- or two-phase class. In a two-phase class, only the combined score will count toward qualifying points. The points are based on the standard ribbon points and are multiplied by the number of competitors. For example: With 16 competitors, first place is 10 points multiplied by $16 = 160$ points. In all two-phase classes, the number is multiplied again by 2: $16 \times 10 \times 2 = 320$.

Jumpers
- Pony Jumpers
- Children's Jumpers
- Junior Jumpers

Approximately thirty of the top point/money earners in these divisions are invited to compete. Check your child's standings on the Web site: www.wihs.org.

THE DEVON HORSE SHOW

The qualifying year for this show is approximately March 31 of one year through April 4 of the next year. One of the most prestigious equestrian events of the year, this show is held each May in Devon, Pennsylvania, and is open to Junior and Pony Hunters by invitation only. Approximately twenty of the top Junior Hunter and thirty of the top Pony Hunter point holders are invited every year, but you must first apply. Points are counted from horse shows beginning by March 31 of the previous year through horse shows beginning by April 4 of the current year, and only the points from your child's most successful fifteen horse shows count. If your child attends more than fifteen, you give Devon a list of the top fifteen.

Keeping track of points to qualify for Devon is the same as keeping track of indoor points, except that the qualifying period is different, so it *is* possible to qualify for Devon in a year that you don't qualify for indoors. The points are verified with USEF, and only when all the entries are in (by the closing date) are the invitations issued. The competition to get invited to Devon is often more fierce than the actual show itself. It is not unknown for parents to be racing to a few more shows than planned come March and early April, just to be sure that their child is still on top. Doing well at Devon not only usually secures a spot at indoors, but also secures a good sale price on the pony or horse once the time comes.

NAYRC: THE NORTH AMERICAN YOUNG RIDERS CHAMPIONSHIPS (JUMPERS ONLY)

Held every year in August, the NAYRC is an international competition that includes the United States, Canada, Mexico, Bermuda, and the

Caribbean Islands. It is considered the Junior Olympics and offers competition in all four of the Olympic sports: Show Jumping, Dressage, Eventing, and Reining. Selection criteria is similar to the Prix des States, with each zone sending a team. Team members are restricted to ages sixteen to twenty-one, and riders must be competing at the Junior Jumper level or above. There are both team and individual competitions. There is also a Junior Young Rider's Championship, for those talented riders under age sixteen, with the selection criteria dictated by each zone.

BET/USET

Qualifying year: September 1 through August 31.

East Coast Finals

Held the first week of October every year in Gladstone, New Jersey. Thirty points are needed to be invited, with at least one of those classes being a 1st place. Points are awarded to the 1st and 2nd place winner in any BET/USET Talent Search Class held at participating horse shows:

1st Place = 10 Points
2nd Place = 5 Points

West Coast Finals

Held in California every year, during the last weekend in September. Thirty points are needed to qualify, but the rules are a little different for the West Coast:

1st Place = 30 Points
2nd Place = 15 Points
3rd Place = 10 Points

BATES USA EQUITATION CHAMPIONSHIP

In addition to the year-end equitation finals, there is also a computer ranking list that awards the top three junior riders for their efforts in a combination of equitation classes. The riders may compete for these spots until they are twenty-one. There is also a year-end final—the Syracuse Invitational—for the top rankers to compete against each other. Information for the finals and the list can be found at www.ryegate.com.

NATIONAL CHILDREN'S MEDAL FINAL

Currently sponsored by Monarch International and held every year in late September at the Capital Challenge Horse Show in Maryland, this final is for the 3' equitation class held at most horse shows. The top thirty (approximately) point holders are invited, and points are earned based on the ribbon points multiplied by the number of competitors.

For example: 1st Place = 10 points x # of competitors in the class = points earned. The points may be earned at any horse show that hosts this class, at any place in the country. The class is open to any junior who has not won the Children's Medal final, or who has not attended a "Big Eq" Final: USEF, Maclay, Washington, USET.

Below is an overview that will give you enough ammunition to understand the workings of the jumpers. Beyond this, there are more tables and further clarification of faults that are listed in the USEF's rule book, Chapter VII.

- **Table II, Sec. 1:** This is a timed "first round"; that is, equally "clean" rounds are placed according to speed, followed by those with faults.
- **Table II, Sec. 2(a):** This class is scored as above, but with a jump-off when the top placings have equal faults. In this case, if there are no clean rounds in the jump-off, the least faults wins, with the fastest speed being the deciding factor if there are equal faults again.
- **Table II, Sec. 2(b):** After the first round, if a competitor has gone "clean," she remains in the ring for the subsequent jump-off. She must wait for the signal to begin. If there is a tie, there will be another jump-off.
- **Table II, Sec. 2(a/b):** Same as above; but if the management allows, the competitor may complete the jump-off at the end of all the other rounds.
- **Table II, Sec. 2(c):** If a competitor goes "clean" in the first round, she continues, without waiting, into the jump-off. A subsequent jump-off will be held for ties for first place.
- **Table II, Sec. 2(d):** In this case, there is a jump-off of a predetermined number of competitors. This can be from six to sixteen, but never more than the number of prizes awarded. This would be stated in the prize list for that particular horse show. Usually, there is an "order of go," which means that for the jump-off, there is a written order, with the last place usually going first. The winner is the winner of the jump-off, no matter where she qualified in the first round.
- **Table II, Sec. 3:** This is held only when there is an equality of faults (or no faults) after the first round and first jump-off. There will be a second jump-off to place the winner.

Appendix II E: The Marshall and Sterling League Finals

Not part of the traditional big "indoors," this is a relatively new final, held for the first time in 2003 with plans to be held every October in Worcester, Massachusetts. The M & S League sponsors finals for Children's and Adult Hunters, Pony Hunters, Open Hunters, the Charles Owen Children's Medal, the HBO Junior Medal, Junior Jumpers, Children's and Adult Jumpers, and Pony Jumpers. It also hosts a Grand Prix.

Points are gained at the more than five hundred horse shows sponsoring M & S Children's (and Adult) Hunter Classics and Jumper Classics. In addition, points may be accrued for the finals for Pony Hunters, either by a Classic or one sponsored class in a Pony Hunter division. The top sixty or so point holders in the Children's and Pony Hunter and Jumper divisions are invited to the finals. Junior Jumpers are invited based on high money earnings, and the top one hundred in the HBO Junior Medal and the top fifty in the Charles Owen Children's Medal are invited to the year-end finals.

M & S Points: Points for the M & S finals are earned for the top six places in a Classic, or the top six places in a sponsored class. Points are the same as ribbon points, with bonus points of ten and six going to the Champion and Reserve, respectively.

Here is a handy chart to copy and use for keeping your M & S records. This chart is good for Children's Hunter and Jumpers, Pony Hunter and Jumpers, and the Charles Owen Children's Medal.

Marshall and Sterling League Record Keeper

	Place						Champion	Reserve	Totals
HS & Date↓	1=10	2=6	3=4	4=2	5=1	6=½	10	6	

The USEA has a point system for year-end awards that changes as competitors move up the levels. The points are based on the overall placing and number of competitors in each level. The points are as follows:

Novice and Training Level Points

Place→	1	2	3	4	5
Number of Competitors↓					
<10	5	4	3	2	1
11–18	6	5	4	3	2
19+	7	6	5	4	3

For instance, if your child is in a horse trial and finishes first overall against nine competitors, she will receive five points toward a year-end placing. Similarly, if she finishes third overall against nineteen other competitors, she will also receive five points toward a year-end placing.

For those competing at Preliminary level and above, the points are based on the USEA/USEF horse grading system that classifies competing event horses according to their competitions (and level of competitions) won. As above, the points for each level are given according to the number of competitors starting the event, and also according to the level of the event (Horse Trial, Two-Day, CCI, etc.). In the 2004 rule book, this grading system can be found on pages 121 and 122. A simple overview of Preliminary and Intermediate levels is included below. Note that 1st through 3rd place are always awarded; 4th through 10th need more than fifteen starters to receive points.

Preliminary Level

Place	Starters	Horse Trial	Two-Day	CIC★	CCI★
1		6	7	8	15
2		5	6	7	12
3		4	5	6	10
4	>15	3	4	5	8
5	>19	2	3	4	7
6	>23	1	2	2	6
7	>27	1	1	2	5
8	>31	1	1	2	4
9	>35	1	1	2	3
10	>37	1	1	2	3

For Preliminary level, points are added for competitors having clean cross-country rounds with no jump penalties: 3 points each for Two-Day Events and CCI★ Events. For example: If your child placed 4th in a Two-Day event with twenty starters, she would receive 3 points for her 4th place, plus 3 points if she had a clean cross-country round, for a total of 6 points.

Intermediate Level

Place	Starters	Horse Trial	Two-Day	CIC★★	CCI★★
1		12	12	16	30
2		10	11	13	28
3		8	9	12	26
4	>15	6	7	10	24
5	>19	4	5	8	22
6	>23	2	3	6	20
7	>27	2	3	6	16
8	>31	2	3	6	16
9	>35	2	3	6	13
10	>37	2	3	6	13

At Intermediate level, points are also added for competitors having clean cross-country rounds (no jump penalties): 5 points each for Two-Day Events and CCI★★ Events. For example: A 3rd place would receive 8 points, with 5 more added for a clean cross-country round, totaling 13 points.

The USEA Web site, www.useventing.com, keeps a current "Leader Board" for the top ten in each level. Go to the Web site and click on "Competitions," and from there go to "Leader Board" to see who is in the lead at any given time.

Year-end awards are given in the following categories (for junior riders): Novice Junior Rider, Training Junior Rider, Preliminary Junior Rider, Intermediate Young Rider, Advanced Rider.

Glossary

Add: This is when the rider adds an entire extra stride in a line of jumps.

Aids: The signals the rider gives to her horse through the seat, hands, and legs. Western riders call them "cues." Spurs and whips are known as artificial aids.

Aiken: A fence with brush on two sides and a rail on top.

ASTM: American Society for Testing and Materials is the organization that tests and designates standards for, among other things, riding helmets. ASTM-approved head gear is deemed to be the safest protection for your child's head in the case of an accident. They are required for hunter/jumper and eventing competitions.

Bank: Not the building where you withdraw all that horse show money. A bank (or embankment) is a steep decline or incline in the land, often with another element at the bottom, such as water, a ditch, or a fence.

Billet: A piece of leather that hooks the saddle to the cinch. Or, what you say to your trainer when you're out of money.

Bosal (pronounced bo-SAL): This unusual-looking piece of tack, with lots of rope and horsehair knots hanging under the horse's chin, is part of a Western bitless bridle.

Breast collar: A piece of tack that goes across the chest of the horse and attaches to both sides of the saddle, to keep the saddle from slipping.

Bullfinch: A cross-country fence that has high brush coming out of the top. The brush is thin, and can be jumped through.

Canter: This is a horse's natural three-beat gait. There are "right" (as in "correct") leads and "wrong" leads which have to do with the horse's balance, and which set of legs precedes the other set. In Western lingo, the canter is a slightly faster version of the lope.

Champion: The winner of a division, determined by adding the number of points the rider gets in each class of her division. See the ribbons and the corresponding points on page 142.

Change of lead: When changing direction at the canter or lope, the horse balances himself by changing the leading leg. This can be done by walking or trotting through the change; when it's done instantly, it's called a flying change.

Chaps: Leather leggings that fit over regular pants or jeans. They are beneficial in their ability to keep one's legs in the saddle and against the horse. They are required in certain Western classes.

Chip: Not a food, not a desired commodity, but plentiful nonetheless. This is when the horse or pony plants a big out-of-sync step or "stride" right in front of the jump. For example, if your child is supposed to ride five strides between two jumps in a line, but she fits in an awkward extra stride, she has "chipped."

Cinch: The belt-like strap that goes around the belly of the horse and attaches to the saddle (via the billet and off billet) to keep the saddle in place. It is called a girth in English riding.

Cinchy: A term for a horse that dislikes being cinched up.

Class: The basic unit of a horse show division.

Coffin: An unseemly name for an obstacle, this consists of a ditch between two fences, with the ground sloping down between the fences toward the ditch.

Coggins test: A blood test to check for Equine Infectious Anemia, a highly contagious and potentially fatal disease. A proof of "negative" Coggins is required by horse shows for all participating horses. A vet performs this test, and the negative results usually cover one year. This paperwork is usually presented to the show office.

Collected: A movement at the trot or canter that results in the horse's stride being shorter and the "frame" of the horse being more compact.

Combination: Certain obstacles (jumps) may be doubled or tripled in a line. Unlike an oxer, these jumps are jumped individually, but the jump is considered a single obstacle with two or more parts or elements, and will be marked, for example, "13, a, b, and c."

Conformation: The way a horse is put together. All breeds have their ideal, so in a conformation class, the judge compares your horse or pony with the ideal type.

Cooler: A wool blanket, often with fancy braided trim, for your child's pony/horse to wear to and from the ring.

Coop: A triangular box jump made to resemble a chicken coop.

Counter-Canter: This is required in more advanced equitation classes. It means going to the right on the left lead, or to the left on the right lead.

Cross-Canter: This is not part of an equitation test. This is when the canter lead of the front leg is different from the lead in back.

Cross-Country: The speed and endurance part of eventing.

Cues: See "Aids."

Diagonal: The rider's posting motion in relation to the horse's footfall at the trot. The rider who rises when the horse's left fore foot and right hind foot strike the ground when the horse is traveling in a counterclockwise direction around the ring is posting on the left diagonal.

Ditch: A depression in a cross-country course. Sometimes a ditch is on the other side of a jump, or it can be between two jumps, so the horse lands from the first jump, jumps the ditch, and immediately jumps another fence.

Division: A group of single classes of the same category.

Dressage: A specific method of training a horse to respond to the rider's aids in such a way that the horse develops its muscles and movements to its best advantage. Dressage is an Olympic competitive discipline in its own right, and is also a one-third component of the eventing discipline.

Drop: When an obstacle (such as a fence) has a landing side lower than the takeoff side. The measurement of the drop is from the top of the fence to the lowest point of the landing side. As for spreads, each level of competing has a parameter for drops.

Element: This is a component of an obstacle, such as an obstacle with water. For example, a fence to be jumped with water on one side.

Exhibitor: Anyone participating in a horse show or event.

Extended: The opposite of collected. A horse's stride is said to be extended when his body is elevated and his legs are stretched out at a controlled pace.

Event: The official name of an eventing competition. Specifically refers to two- and three-day events, but may be used casually in reference to mini-events (an unrecognized schooling type competition), tests, horse trials, or Pony Club rallies.

Fences: These are the obstacles to be jumped. A complete list of show-jumping fences can be found in the hunter/jumper chapter (Chapter 9, page 114).

Figures: In a dressage test, figures are required elements such as circles, half-circles, serpentines, and figure eights.

Flying change: A change of lead at the lope or canter, in one coordinated motion. Many classes, such as Western Riding and Hunter, require one or more flying lead changes.

Forehand: The part of the horse in front of the saddle. Usually used in relation to a required movement, as in "a turn on the forehand," which requires the horse to use his hind legs to circle around while his front legs stay in place.

Formal attire: Not an evening gown, and not for you, Mom. Some classes either suggest or require formal attire. Formal attire for a Hunter Classic would require a shadbelly coat (black or navy). A Jumper Classic would require a hunt-type jacket. Although not required, white breeches are normally worn. Dressage formal attire includes a top hat, shadbelly coat, and white breeches.

Freestyle: A type of dressage test, freestyle is a choreographed dressage "dance" with required movements, set to music. Also referred to as "kur" (German for *choice*).

Gaits: The horse's different pace of forward movements: walk, trot, canter, gallop.

Hack: This is a crossover term with a different meaning in each discipline. In Western lingo, a hunter "hack" is a type of horse well suited to the hunter classes. It is also the name of a class that includes jumping two fences and demonstrating a flying change of lead. In the hunter/jumper world, a hunter hack is a flat class only.

Half-Pass: The horse moves sideways and forward at the same time, its head bent slightly in the direction of the sideways movement.

Halter: Both a type of class at a horse show and a piece of tack-like equipment. A halter restrains a riderless horse and is used in place of a bridle in this instance. A horse shown in a "halter" class is judged on its conformation.

Hands: Based on an approximation of a big man's fist (four inches across the back), all ponies and horses are measured in a combination of hands and inches. A 13.1 hand pony is 53" tall. The measurement is from the ground to the top of the pony's withers.

Headstall: The part of the bridle worn over the horse's head to keep the bit in his mouth. Not a hole in the wall for a horse's head.

Hock: It bends the horse's hind leg joint, the equivalent of the human knee.

Horsemanship: A class at a Western show (not to be confused with the talent needed to compete in this class).

Hog's back: A triple oxer—three jumps pushed together with the middle jump being the highest. (Imagination helps.)

Horse trial: A type of event, qualifying one to participate at three-day events.

Hunter: A "type," not breed, of horse that simulates a foxhunter's mount.

Impulsion: A favorite and oft-used dressage term; describes the desired "motor" the horse can use at the trot and canter. It's never about speed, but about the energy contained in the movements.

In-and-Out: One of the few names that make sense. Two jumps in a row where the horse jumps in, lands, takes one or two strides, and jumps out. A one-stride in-and-out should not be done in two strides.

Jog: The trot in Western lingo. Also, a somewhat slower and more rhythmic version than its English riding counterpart. In a hunter class, the judge may ask a horse to "jog," or be trotted, to check for its soundness.

Jump out: Showing out of your horse trailer for a day. The horse stays tied up by the trailer and doesn't require a stall.

Keyhole: Usually made with brush, this obstacle is a hole that the horse and rider jump through. This is only seen at the higher levels.

Latigo: Long strips of leather used in Western tack, most often to secure rain slickers to the back of a working horse saddle.

Lead: This term has many uses. It literally means to "direct" a horse. It also refers to the rope or leather strap that attaches to the halter (also called "lead shank"). It can mean the way in which the horse properly balances himself at the canter when going in each direction. In the simplest terms, when going to the left, the left foreleg (inside leg) and left inside hind leg are leading or moving farther forward than their outside counterparts.

Leg yield: Using the leg to push a horse to move to the side while maintaining a forward direction. The horse's legs cross over beneath him.

Liverpool: A water jump, typically a blue mat on the ground adjacent to the fence; occasionally, it does contain water.

Lope: The canter in Western lingo; also, a slower version of its English counterpart.

On the flat: Usually an equitation class, "on the flat" is just that—no jumping.

Obstacle: This is the catch-all term given to arena jumps, cross-country jumps, mounds, ditches, etc. In cross-country, obstacles must be marked by red and white flags, with the red on the right and white on the left.

Oxer: A jump compound of two or three elements to test a horse's ability to jump width. The spread (distance between the two jumps) is related to the height of the jumps. The higher the jumps, the wider the spread. The name actually does refer to oxen, who, although they *can* jump fences, are reluctant to do so if the fences are wide. Pasture fences for cows and oxen are often doubled for this reason.

Passage (sounds like massage): An advanced dressage movement required at Intermediate II and higher. Beautiful, airy, and dreamlike suspended motion at the trot.

Pattern: The required movements in a class where the rider or handler is being judged. It is often marked with orange cones to indicate transition points.

Piaffe: Another dressage movement required at Intermediate II and above, this is a trot in place or on the spot. Think of the horse dancing in place.

Pin, pinning, pinned: A ribbon, getting a ribbon, having gotten a ribbon. Not normally pinned on anything—occasionally hung from the horse's bridle—but handed out to the top six, eight or ten riders, depending upon the class.

Pirouette: Performed at the canter, this beautiful dressage movement asks the horse to circle on its forehand while simply pivoting on one of its hind legs.

Poll: Different, indeed, from a "pole" on the ground used in speed classes. The "poll" is the highest point of the horse's head, right behind the ears.

Posting trot: In English classes, the rider rises and sits with the motion of the horse's trot.

Prize list: The horse show booklet that includes an entry form and lists the classes offered, suggestions for local hotels, a map, and other useful information.

Rein-back: Asking the horse to move backwards.

Renvers: A dressage movement where the horse travels with hindquarters bent toward the rail or outside, and with the shoulders and head traveling straight ahead.

Reserve: One spot past the last ribbon given out. In a class pinned to six places, reserve would be seventh place.

Reserve Champion: A division's second-place winner.

Rollback turn: A 180-degree hairpin turn to a jump going the other way from the previously jumped fence.

Sanctioned: An officially recognized show venue, which means that points count and accrue toward year-end awards.

Set up: In Western classes, getting a horse to stand squarely on all four feet.

Shadbelly: A formal coat worn in a Hunter Classic or by dressage riders at the upper levels. It comes in black or navy and is double-breasted with tails.

Shank and lead shank: The rope attached to a halter for leading a horse; sometimes has a chain section that can be put over the nose of an unruly horse or under the chin in Showmanship classes.

Shoulder in: A movement where the horse's front end is bent toward the inside of the track as it moves forward while its inside hind leg is on the same track as the outside foreleg.

Showmanship: Generically, "showmanship" is the ability to get people's attention with one's style or skill, a necessary component of every competitive equine sport. However, in Western lingo, this means only one thing: a specific class in which the handler's ability is judged.

Steeplechase: Historically deriving its name from an informal race across country toward a church steeple, the steeplechase (in itself its own racing discipline) is a speed race over brush obstacles, carried out at a gallop.

Soundness: An absence of lameness.

Spread: This is the distance across a jump or obstacle. Spreads are measured from the highest point of a jump—the base—or across an obstacle without height, such as water. Each level of competition has parameters for spread lengths.

Stride: One complete horse step at the trot or canter.

Suppleness: Flexibility and smoothness of movement rolled into one tidy expression.

Swap: This is a "changed" flying lead on the way to a jump. Horses and ponies will often do so on their own to rebalance themselves. Judges have varying opinions on this, but there are times when it always results in a markdown.

Swedish Oxer: Poles are set at an angle to each other on the opposite standards, forming an "X."

Tempi: Referring to timed changes of lead called "tempi changes." Advanced-level dressage tests require changes of lead to occur every four strides, then two strides, then every stride. The strides are often referred to as "beats." It's a beautiful thing to watch.

Test: A required set of movements for any particular class at a horse show. In Western classes, a test is usually called a "pattern." In eventing, a test is one aspect of an event or horse trial.

Throughness: Like suppleness, but an expression that more specifically describes the ability of the horse to respond throughout his body to the rider's aid.

Trakehner: A type of cross-country obstacle which consists of a fence set into a ditch.

Travers: An advanced dressage movement where the horse travels forward with shoulder to the wall or outside and hindquarters to the inside.

Triple bar: Three jumps pushed together with ascending heights, front to back.

Trot: A two-beat gait. The English version of the Western jog, the trot has longer strides and is often faster than the jog.

USEF: United States Equestrian Federation, this country's regulatory organization for domestic and international equestrian competition, formed in 2004 by the merger of the American Horse Shows Association and the United States Equestrian Team.

Vertical: A fence composed of a single element, to a test a horse's ability to jump height.

Volte: A small (6-, 8-, or 10-meter) circle performed in dressage.

Water Elements: A brook or small pool of water. In show jumping, an artificial pool of water is known as a Liverpool.

Wings: Structures next to a jump standard to give the jump a more solid look.

Withers: The highest point between the horse's back and neck.

Wrong lead: Cantering on the incorrect lead, such as the right foreleg and hind leg preceding the left ones when the horse is cantering to the left.

Resources

Books

American Quarter Horse Association Official Handbook of Rules and Regulations (52nd edition). American Quarter Horse Association, 2004.

DeWitt, Kitti. *Whinny Widget: Instructors' Dressage Test Book*. 2002.

Montague, Sarah and P. J. Dempsey. *The Complete Idiot's Guide to Horses*. Indianapolis: Alpha Books, 2003.

Morris, George H. *Hunter Seat Equitation*. Garden City: Doubleday & Company, 1971.

Pavia, Audrey with Janice Posnikoff, DVM. *Horses for Dummies*. New York: Hungry Minds, Inc., 1999.

Pinto Horse Association of America Official Rule Book. Pinto Horse Association of America, Inc., 2003.

Pony of the Americas Club Official Handbook. Pony of the Americas Club, Inc., 2002.

Price, Steven D. *The Horseman's Illustrated Dictionary*. New York: The Lyons Press, 2000.

Shrake, Richard with Pat Close. *Western Horsemanship*. Colorado Springs: Western Horseman, Inc., 2001.

Watson, Gill. *A Young Person's Guide to Eventing*. Warwickshire: The Pony Club, 1999.

White-Mullin, Anna Jane. *Winning: A Training and Showing Guide for Hunter Seat Riders*. North Pomfret: Trafalgar Square Publishing, 1992.

Periodicals

The Chronicle of the Horse (www.chronofhorse.com)

Dressage Today. Primedia, Inc.

Equestrian. USA Equestrian.

EQUUS. Primedia, Inc.

Horse & Rider. Primedia, Inc.

USDF Connection. United States Dressage Federation.

Web Sites:

www.apha.com (American Paint Horse Association)

www.appaloosa.com (Appaloosa Horse Club)

www.aqha.com (American Quarter Horse Association)

www.arabianhorses.org (Arabian Horse Association)

www.equisearch.com (EquiSearch, Primedia, Inc.)

www.eventingusa.com (United States Eventing Association)

www.nhs.org (National Horse Show Association of America)

www.pinto.org (Pinto Horse Association of America)

www.poac.org (Pony of the Americas Club)

www.ryegate.com (Ryegate Show Services, Inc.)

www.usef.org (United States Equestrian Federation)

www.wihs.org (The Washington International Horse Show)

A

Age qualifications, 84–85, 121
  dressage, 160
  equitation, 134, 135
  eventing, 174, 188
  hunters, 130–131
Aids, 83, 148, 243
All American Quarter Horse
  Congress, 103–104
American Eventing
  Championship, 189–190
American Paint Horse, 80
American Paint Horse
  Association (APHA), 80
  membership fees, 85
  points/awards, 106–107,
    201–203
  shows, 104
American Quarter Horse, 80
American Quarter Horse
  Association (AQHA), 80
  membership fees, 85
  points/awards, 106, 197–200
  shows, 103–104
American Society for Testing &
  Materials (ASTM), 243
Annual Youth Arabian
  Championship Horse Show,
  105
Appaloosa Horse Club (ApHC)
  membership fees, 85
  points/awards, 107–108,
    205–206
  shows, 104

Appaloosas, 80
AQHA Youth World Show, 103
Arabian Horse Association
  (AHA)
  membership fees, 85
  points/awards, 109–110, 215
  shows, 105
Arabians, 80
Awards. See specific associations

B

Barn, 21–34
  barn family, 25–27
  and finances, 27–29
  levels of riders, 30–31
  parent's role at, 31–34
  requirements for, 21–23
  safety in, 24
  and show schedules, 29–30
Barrels, 100
Basic Life Support, 24
Bate, Kendall, **36**
Bates USA Equitation
  Championship, 232
Belt, 86
Booth, Samantha, **162**
Boots, 86
  dressage, 153
  English outfit, 90
  hunter/jumpers, 122
Boys, clothing for, 87
Brannaman, Buck, 40
Breeches, 121–122
British Pony Club, 169

C
Canadian National Arabian
   Championship Horse Show,
   105
Canter, 83, 112, 148, 243
   change of lead, 148, 243, 246
   collected, 170, 244
   counter-canter, 149, 244
   cross-canter, 245
   extended, 245
   impulsion, 150
   stride, 118
   wrong lead, 118
Chaps, 82, 244
Child. *See* Rider
Chip, 112, 244
Clinics, 41–42
Clothing, 12–13
   dressage, 152–154
   English riding, **89,** 90
   eventing, 174–177
   formal attire, 118, 126, 246, 249
   hunter/jumpers, 121–127
   trainer's guidelines for, 37
   Western, 85–89
Coats
   dressage, 152
   hunt, 90
   shadbelly, 118, 126, 127, 249
Coggins test, 6, 244
Commissions, trainer's, 54–57
Conformation, 82, 244
   Halter class, 91
Costs, 27–29, 43–44, 193–194
   buying horse, 53–59
   memberships, 85, 120, 152, 174

for rated shows, 7–8
for schooling shows, 4, 5
selling horse, 61
for trainers, 37
Cross-country, 170
   clothing for, 175
   scoring, 185–186
Cues. *See also* Aids, 83

D
Daniels, Chétie, **64**
Devon Horse Show, 231
Disciplines, equestrian. *See also*
      specific disciplines, 1, 3
   judging in, 68, 72
   rated shows, 6–8
Dressage, 3, 147–165, 170–171,
   245
   awards, 163–165
   clothing, 152–154, 176
   freestyle, 149, 150, 159, 246
   glossary, 148–151
   judging, 68, 70, 155–156
   levels in, 156–159
   movements in, 170, 244, 246,
      247, 248, 249, 250
   resources for, 165
   scoring, 186–187
   shows, 159–163
   tests in, 154–155
Driving, 3
Drugs, testing horse, 58

E
Endurance riding, 3
English riding, 3, 6

clothing for, **89,** 90
  hunt seat equitation, 98–99
Equine Infectious Anemia (EIA),
    6, 244
Equitation, 80, 111, 119
  clothing, 121, 122
  divisions in, 133–138
  dressage equitation, 161–162
  on the flat, 118
  hunt seat, 98–99
  points, 224
  resources for, 145–146
  shows, 227–228, 229–230,
    232–233
Event, 90, 170
Eventing, 3, 167–192
  clothing, 174–177
  glossary, 170–173
  horse trials, 178–181
  levels, 181–184, 188
  memberships/age
    qualifications, 173–174
  national competitions, 189–191
  resources, 191–192
  safety in, 180–181
  scoring/points, 184–187, 188,
    239–241
  tests, 177–178
  year-end awards, 188–189

F
Fathers, 73–78
Fédération Equestre
    Internationale, 158–159 163
Fences, 112, 245
  glossary, 114–116

Food, 14–17

G
Gaits. *See also* specific gaits, 83,
    112, 118, 245
Gallop, 112
Garters, 125
Girls, Western clothing. *See also*
    Clothing, 87–89
Glazer, Elizabeth, **125**
Glazer, Kelsey, **30, 125**
Glazer, Sydney, **30**
Glossary, 243–250
  dressage, 148–151
  eventing, 170–173
  hunter/jumper, 112–118
  Western, 82–84
Gloves, 90, 124

H
Hack, 83, 246
Halter class, 91–92, 246
Halter (tack), 83, 246
Hats. *See also* Helmets, 86, 153
Health certificates, horse's, 6
Helmets, 90, 123–124, 243
  dressage, 153–154
Horsemanship class, 80, 97, **98**
  clothing, 89
Horses
  barn requirements, 21–24
  bonding with, 59–60
  buying, 38, 53–59
  classroom sessions on, 42–43
  conformation, 70, **71,** 82, 244
  costs of, 193–194

Horses (continued)
  events judging, 90–96
  forehand, 83, 149, 246
  gaits/movements of, 82, 83,
    112, 118, 148–149, 150, 151,
    245
  hack type, 83, 246
  hunter type, 83, 128–129
  keeping at home, 24–25
  measurement of, 117, 246
  poll, 84, 248
  recording fees, 120, 174
  selling, 60–65
  Western breeds, 79–80
  withers, 250
Horse shows. See also specific
    shows, associations, 1, 3–4,
    9–20
  dressage, 159–163
  equitation, 133–138
  eventing, 177–180, 189–191
  events judging horses, 90–96
  events judging rider, 96–100
  food at, 14–17
  hunter/jumpers, 127–133,
    138–141
  indoors/other national shows,
    227–233, 237
  judging, 67–72
  "jump-out," 3, 83
  parents' role at, 17–20, 73–78
  points in, 101–103, 197–215
  prize list/entry form, 118,
    120–121, 248
  rated/non-rated, 6–8, 84–85,
    127–128
  schooling shows, 4–6

  speed events, 100–101
  Western breed, 79–80, 103–105
  what to bring, 10–13
Horse trials, 171, 178–181
  levels, 181–184
Hunt coat, 90
Hunter/Jumpers, 111–146
  basic facts, 119–121
  clothing for, 121–127
  finals/year-end awards, 143–145
  glossary, 112–118
  hunters' divisions, 128–133
  jumpers' divisions, 138, 140–141
  jumpers' scoring, 139–140
  organizations, 217
  points, 142–143, 219–223,
    225–226
  rated divisions, 127–128
  resources for, 145–146
  shows, 227–229, 230, 231
Hunter type. See also
    Hunter/Jumpers, 83, 247
  classes of, 94–96
Hunt Seat Equitation class, 98–99

I
Impulsion, 150
International Show, 105

J
Jackets, 122, 126–127, 249
Jodhpurs, 121
Jog, 83, 84, 118, 247
Judging. See also Points, 67–72
  dressage, 155–156
  equitation, 133–138
  horse, 70, **71,** 90–96

hunter types, 128–129
points in, 101–103
rider, 96–100
in schooling shows, 4–5
speed events, 100–101
subjectivity in, 68
Jumpers. *See also* Hunter/Jumpers
divisions in, 140–141
prize money, 140
scoring, 139–140
shows, 228–229, 230, 231–232
tables, 235
Jumping. *See* Hunter/Jumpers;
Show jumping

K
Kart, Brittany, **177**

L
Lead, 83, 118, 247
change of, 82, 112, 148, 243
flying change, 246
lead shank, 249
swap, 250
wrong lead, 84, 250
Leadline class, 99–100
Leone, Peter, **39**
Lieb, Toby, 17
Lope. *See also* Canter, 83, 248
Lyons, John, 40

M
Maffit Lake Farm, **34**
Marshall and Sterling League,
138, 217
finals, 131, 237–238
May, Alex, **124**

McLean, Brian, **74**
McLean, Hanna, **74**
Memberships. *See* specific
associations
Morgans, 80
Murray, Jacque, **81, 99**
Murray, Marylynn, **99**
Murray, Sylvia, **88, 91**

N
National Children's Medal Final,
233
National Horse Show (NHS),
217, 229–230
Nation Reining Horse
Association (NRHA), 92
North American League (NAL),
217, 225
championship, 228–229
North American Young Riders
Championship (NAYRC),
158, 162–163, 189, 231–232

O
Obstacles, 171–173, 248
combination, 170, 244
fences, 112, 114–116, 245
spread, 249
Olympics, 3
NAYRC, 231–232
Organizations, breed. *See also*
specific associations
and sanctioned shows, 6, 84–85
Western breeds, 80

P
Paint-O-Ramas, 104

Paint World, 104
Palominos, 80
Pants, 86
   for dressage, 153
   English outfit, 90
   hunter/jumpers class, 121–122
Parelli, Pat, 40
Parents
   fathers, 73–78
   role at shows, 17–20
   role in barn, 31–34
   and trainers, 38–39, 44–51
Pattern, 84 ·
Paxton, Shannon, **87, 98, 102**
Pennsylvania National Horse
   Show, 227–228
Pessoa, Rodrigo, **126**
Pinto Horse Association of
   America (PtHA)
   membership fees, 85
   points/awards, 198–109,
      211–213
   show, 105
Pintos, 80
Points
   AHA's rules, 215
   APHA's rules, 201–203
   ApHC's rules, 205–206
   AQHA's rules, 197–200
   champion, 112
   equitation, 224
   eventing, 239–241
   hunter/jumpers, 142–143,
      219–223, 225–226
   Marshall and Sterling League
      finals, 237–238
   POAC's rules, 207–208

PtHA's rules, 211
   Western breeds, 92, 93–96, 101,
      103
Pole bending, 100
Ponies. *See* Horses
Pony Club. *See also* Eventing, 167,
   168–169
Pony of the Americas, 80
Pony of the Americas Club
   (POAC)
   membership fees, 85
   points/awards, 108, 207–209
   shows, 104–105
Publications, 251–252
   dressage, 165
   eventing, 192
   hunter/jumper, 145
   Western breeds, 110

R
R. W. Mutch Foundation
   Equitation Scholarship, 146
"Ratcatcher" shirt, 90
Reining, 3, 92–93
Resources, 251–252
   dressage, 165
   eventing, 191–192
   hunter/jumpers, 145–146
   Western breeds, 110
Ribbons. *See also* Scoring; Points,
   101, 118
   and points, 142
Rider
   age qualifications, 84–85, 121,
      130–131, 160, 174, 188
   aids, 148, 243
   and barn family, 25–27